Richard III

Gail

Cathy

Willie

log of the molly brown

By Richard Zantzinger

Westover
Publishing Company

A Media General Publication   Richmond, Virginia

Illustrated by Wayne Barrett

ACKNOWLEDGEMENT

I am not a writer—an adventurous small boat captain yes, and to some degree a teller of tales—but a writer no. The ideas and the interest were there to recount an unusual and humorous sea story, but my novice pen suffered the lack of an inspired muse to put experiences and thoughts on paper. It was Wayne Barrett whose enthusiasm for the story encouraged my continued efforts, and whose guidance and creativity as an editor produced the end result. Had it not been for Wayne Barrett's experienced professional eye—his ability to sift through rough manuscript pages, sketchy log entries and my verbalized commentary to capture with style the essence of the tale and the personalities involved—this ''warped, faded, frayed log book'' would have remained buried forever in some moldy locker.

DEDICATION

Kyle and Richard Zantzinger

Dick

Preface

Memory is an imperfect commodity full of distortions and omissions. Things you think you'll remember you forget, and trivial stuff you don't give a damn about seems to linger in your brain forever. After awhile, especially after a long while, what was real gets mixed up with imagination or with something you've read or heard. That's why some people who write their memoirs end up telling lies. They probe their memories, take a snippet here, a scrap there, then ladle on the fiction. While I'm not very old and not famous—except maybe to several kids and a Polynesian railroader—I tell a story that reads like fiction, but isn't. That's because it was written as things happened or didn't happen.

This is not to say the *Log of Molly Brown* is complete in itself. I felt some things didn't properly belong in that tattered old record book. They do belong in this narrative; so trust my memory that, for instance, I knew which girl it was I went skinny-dipping with in Bali. But mainly my story is taken from the log. Not all of the log, of course. I don't recount the wind speed or what I ate at breakfast every day. On the other hand, I expand on some entries—for your benefit, not mine—so now they don't read quite so much like 90-cent telegrams. The result is either a souped-up or watered-down log. You decide.

Warped, swollen, brittle, faded, frayed at the edges, that logbook looks to be 50 years older than it is. The cloth binding, once grassy green, has been bleached by equatorial sun and salt spray to the color of dried moss. The spine has come unglued, and the pages hang from it by cheeseclothy threads. The blue-lined paper is stained and smudged, even on pages spattered by beer, which I sipped while I wrote when I had it, but the crabbed writing still remains legible. Not all of it is mine, I confess. Toward the end of the log some of the words were put down by an English girl. The log begins about a year before I met her—on July 2, 1969, when I left Key West heading for the Canal Zone. But my story doesn't start there, nor does it begin on that day of goodbyes in June when I sailed out of my home port, Annapolis. I didn't keep a log then because at first I thought it should be more a navigational record than a journal. And since I planned to stick to the Intercoastal Waterway for most of the distance, there wouldn't be much navigating to record. Besides, I didn't have the gall to begin a log of a voyage around the world while playing follow-the-leader down a canal. Hell, I thought, I might not make it as far as Key West. And it wasn't easy.

My story begins, therefore, not with the log, nor the departure, but with me lying in bed while somebody tries to batter down my front door. Thus a beginning, anyway a prologue.

PROLOGUE

In addition to being a good friend, Luke Farley was general superintendent and vice-president of R. C. Zantzinger, Jr., Inc., Concrete Contractor. He had been trying to phone me since eight o'clock—it was now noon—but I wasn't taking any calls or answering any knocks on the door. I simply didn't have the guts to face the day. Luke and I sat at my dining table and traded bad news over cups of coffee. He told me things were at a standstill, that our supplier wouldn't let us have any more concrete until we paid our bill. I said there wasn't enough money in our account to pay it. There wasn't even enough to meet this week's payroll. "We've had it, Luke," I said.

For four years Luke and I had worked hard to keep the business going. Bad luck dogged us—rotten weather, equipment breakdowns, tight money, a hundred other things. Desperate for a big contract to pull us out of the hole, I bid way low to get the concrete work on a school. I left $40,000 on the table. Finally, I scraped enough together to finish the school job. Unwittingly, I had made a generous contribution to an institution of learning. Men have done less for Ph.D.'s.

My situation couldn't have been worse—but was. My marriage had ended in divorce, and I owed a lot of money to the Internal Revenue Service (the main reason I was leery of knocks on the door).

But did I feel sorry for myself? Yes, very. So, you see, the round-the-world idea was a welcome distraction. It was, in fact, absolutely necessary. Connie Whittet, a girl I was dating, suggested it. She spoke in jest. Nevertheless, her remark hit home. For the next days and weeks and months I couldn't get the crazy idea out of my head.

Born and raised in southern Maryland, I had been around boats all my life. Chesapeake Bay was my playground. Sailing was my passion. Why shouldn't I go to sea? All I needed were a boat and a knowledge of navigation.

Within six months I had acquired them. And with a sale of some securities, my financial situation brightened. I satisfied all my creditors except one—the Internal Revenue Service. Looking back, I realize I should have been more concerned about those back taxes, but the prospect of an ocean voyage crowded unpleasant thoughts out of my mind. Besides, my mind had all it could handle in the correspondence course I was taking—18 lessons on celestial navigation.

When I wasn't aiming at the sun, I was looking at boats and listening to yacht brokers. I knew what I wanted: a 35-foot fiberglass, masthead sloop with a diesel engine. The brokers, though they didn't know any more about ocean cruising than I did, tried to sell me a much larger boat, like a double-ended yawl or an ocean-going ketch.

Three days before Christmas, Dave Frey called me. He had owned the kind of boat I had in mind—I had crewed on it—and knew where there was one like it for sale. That was Jim Mercerau's *Son Ceri* berthed at Gibson Island, a little ways up the bay. I drove there Christmas Eve and bought her for $15,500. Though she didn't have a diesel engine, she looked better to me than new boats I had seen at twice the money.

Jim and I shook hands on the deal over a drink of bourbon. He asked if I had a name for the boat. "Yes," I replied. "Molly Brown."

That night I drove to Connie's apartment in Georgetown. She would be delighted to see that in one bold, positive step, I had climbed out of the doldrums and grasped a piece of the future—and all because of her inspired idea. But do you know what she said? She said that I was a jerk to think I could circle the globe by myself in a flimsy sailboat. So I invited her to make the trip with me. She declined.

Although I didn't anticipate sailing 30,000 miles alone, the prospect didn't bother me. With a self-steering rig and a little luck, I felt I could make it. If, on the other hand, the going got rough I could always sell the boat and fly home. That, of course, presupposed an eventuality conveniently taking place in a busy port full of eager buyers and 707's. The possibility that I might have to call it quits on some deserted Pacific atoll didn't occur to me. You think too much about what can happen and you won't even get out of bed. I know.

Having bought *Molly Brown*, nothing now could dissuade me from attempting the trip. It would take at least a year to complete; I didn't have enough money to stretch it out much more than that. Nor did I care to be away too long from my daughter, Kyle, seven, and my son, Richard, five. Kyle, I hoped, might be permitted to travel down the Intercoastal Waterway with me. When the time was ripe, I would ask Boots, my ex-wife.

The possibility of having Kyle along helped me decide when to leave: in June, after school was out. That gave me almost six months to equip *Molly Brown*, bone up on navigation, and chart my course. If I stuck reasonably close to schedule, I figured to be back in Annapolis by late summer of 1970. Buoyed by my experience, I would dutifully go back to work. At what, I didn't know; certainly not the concrete game. As for writing a book, that wouldn't dawn on me until months after my return. Then I would discover it was already written—a hell of a lot of it, anyway—in my beat-up log.

So June it was I planned to leave. At the U.S. Naval Oceanographic Office in Suitland, Maryland, I bought pilot charts, which show wind speed and direction at various times of the year, and plotted a course around the waist of the world to take advantage of trade winds and equatorial currents. The charts told me I had a fair chance of reaching the Cape of Good Hope the following March. Only one thing wrong with that: I would be on a collision course with monsoon winds that might be churning up in the Indian Ocean.

Because of ice in the harbor, I couldn't move the boat from Gibson Island right away. When the ice finally broke, on January 3, I damned near couldn't start her. It took all morning. After lashing the mast, which was out of her, to the cabin, I motored the ten or so miles to Spa Creek, where I tied her up behind my apartment. I remember that mini-maiden voyage well. I thought I would freeze to death before it ended.

But a little cold weather—or a lot of it, as was actually the case—couldn't keep me off the boat. With a borrowed electric heater warming the cabin, I began taking *Molly Brown* apart and putting her back together. To save money, I decided against installing a diesel, choosing instead to overhaul the gasoline engine. Unaccountably, I didn't check out the gas tank. I did get rid of the boat's 15-amp generator, replacing it with a 60-amp alternator serviced by two 150-amp truck batteries. I added bookshelves, reworked the galley, and made compartments for the sextant and other navigational equipment. To create more room in the galley and provide a small space for navigating, I tore out the companionway ladder and put in a folding step. New items I ordered included a Bendix radio direction finder, a sonar 150-watt radio telephone, and a Hasler self-steerer, due to arrive from England in April.

I did not have a sextant, and was advertising in the Annapolis paper for a used one. After a week I forgot about the ad, since it had produced no calls. Then one morning the telephone rang and a female voice asked, "What is that sex thing?" I assured her I didn't know what she was talking about. "That sex thing you advertised for in the paper," she elaborated. A sextant, I explained to her, was a navigational instrument that sailors at sea use to find their position, and did she have one? "No," she said, "I just wanted to know what that thing was," and hung up. Now that she knew, I canceled the ad and bought a new Plath.

Molly Brown came with a good inventory of sails: two spinnakers, drifter, spinnaker staysail, No. 1 genoa, working jib, storm mainsail. Her nine-ounce mainsail made a beautiful round-the-world main. I bought a No. 2 genoa and added two jib halyards, the only changes I made to the running rigging. The standing rigging checked out fine as was. That still left me with a sizable shopping list: 35-pound plow anchor, 100 feet of chain, 40-fathom anchor rodes, sea anchor, kerosene running lights and cabin lights, and extra blocks, shackles, halyards.

The self-steerer arrived April 15. I motored *Molly Brown* to Arnie Gay's Boatyard to have Col. H. G. Hasler's ingenious wind-vane device installed. Attached to the tiller the self-steerer is designed to do just that—keep the boat on course unattended. Thus, if sailing solo, I could sleep and still keep going in the direction desired.

While she was in the yard, I had *Molly Brown*'s bottom painted and larger drains put in the cockpit. Except for charts and stores, the boat was ready to go by the first of May. I had her out almost every day, getting the feel of her, so to speak, and liking what I felt, although the self-steerer gave me some trouble. Downwind with a fresh breeze on the quarter, the boat would wander as much as 90 degrees. In late May, with Connie's parents aboard, we sailed across the bay to St. Michael's, on Maryland's Eastern Shore. I had the self-steerer working better now, though it did jibe the main boom a couple of times.

The following day at noon we left with a brisk breeze blowing out of the northwest. This would be a good test for the self-steerer. I would have to beat out of Miles River into Eastern Bay with the wind right on the nose. I reefed the mainsail, set a small headsail, hooked up the self-steerer, and sailed into the choppy waters. The boat handled beautifully. The wind died down some, but I left the sail shortened. By now, I was beginning to realize the self-steerer functioned best this way.

There was only one mishap on the return trip. My new sextant fell out of its compartment with an expensive-sounding crash. I had forgotten to make it fast with shock cord.

After I bought *Molly Brown* and set about outfitting her, friends began wondering what I was up to. I let them wonder. Sure as hell they would try to talk me out of it if I told them. I hinted now and then that I might take a cruise in the Caribbean, maybe cut through the Panama Canal and taste a little of the Pacific. And, for all I knew, that might be all I wanted. No use talking now and having to eat a lot of leftover words later. But, you know, they—my friends and relatives—still tried to talk me out of going wherever I was going. For instance, one night over a bottle of bourbon, my old friend Bill Addison spent an hour telling me I was running away, I was deserting my children, I did not know what I was doing. Why, he said, I might never be heard from again; stay in southern Maryland, boy, where you belong. His wife Mary suggested that I get a job in a gas station. When they were both through, I asked them if I could take their oldest son Billy with me as crew. I can still hear the door slamming.

A month later, as *Molly Brown* pulled away from waving friends and relatives on the dock, Billy Addison

Kyle

was aboard. So was Kyle; her mother agreed to let her go as far as Key West. Also on board were Connie's brother Robert and his friend Howard Jennings, both just graduated from the University of Virginia. They would accompany me to Panama. Billy planned to get off in Key West with Kyle. But I had gotten passports for all hands, just in case.

We sailed out of Annapolis on June 9, 1969, at 2 P.M. Within an hour we had raised Thomas Point light, about six miles down the bay. There we turned around and sailed back to Annapolis. Kyle had forgotten her bag of clothes.

At 4 P.M. we again got underway, this time for keeps. By next evening we had passed Norfolk, Virginia, and entered the Intercoastal Waterway. After getting through the first lock in the Dismal Swamp, we tied up for the night. Soon we had charcoal glowing in a grill suspended from a ratchet over the stern. Bill made the sauce, I barbecued the chicken, and we all licked our fingers.

It was a picnic all the way to Morehead City, North Carolina. Four days out of Annapolis, the party ended. We headed for open water, challenging the Gulf Stream and my skill as a navigator. Our destination was Fort Lauderdale, Florida, more than 500 nautical miles distant. I estimated, if all went well, we could make it in six days. Instead, everything went wrong, and we missed our target by 400 miles. Here's how it happened.

At twilight on June 13 I broke out the sextant and tried for a star fix, but by the time I identified the stars I wanted to shoot, darkness had blotted out the horizon. I had struck out on my first attempt at celestial navigation. Later that evening, Robert Whittet tried to get a radio fix, and he struck out too. At 3 A.M. a breeze out of the northeast freshened. We shortened sail. By daybreak, the wind was blowing harder, so we dropped the main, going on the working jib alone. I tried for a star fix and failed again. At noon I aimed the sextant at the sun but couldn't keep it on the horizon. Robert's attempt at radio fixes produced nothing but static. However, that told me something. Since our RDF wouldn't pick up a signal from beyond 100 miles, we were at least that far from a radio coastal beacon. Though I didn't know our position, I wasn't too worried; we still had our compass and could dead reckon a course by that. But not for long. During the night a hatch board, torn loose by heavy seas, smashed the compass. We had a spare, which helped not at all, for it read 25 degrees differently from the other. I didn't know which to trust. A week out of Annapolis and we were lost on the Atlantic.

By morning the seas were higher than ever. I had never seen anything like them. When *Molly Brown* was in a trough, the crests reached above the spreaders. If I ever had any doubts that she was a seaworthy boat, she erased them that day. Biting into those mountains of water, she would rise to the top while the seas rolled under her. It was a fascinating experience—so much so, I almost forgot we didn't know where we were. My crew, despite having lost their appetites, seemed to be enjoying themselves. Especially Kyle. Secured by a safety harness, she would lean out of the cockpit and watch the big waves roll in.

At noon I again tried to get a reading for latitude, and again failed. It wasn't a question of not knowing what to do; it was simply a matter of not being able to do it in those heavy seas. Obviously I needed experience. I was getting it—the hard way. Well, to hell with this, I thought; we have to get out of the Gulf Stream and into calmer waters. That meant heading westward toward the coast. But which way was west? The setting sun told me. I took dead aim on it and held *Molly Brown* to that course. We awoke next morning to a subdued sea and a gentle breeze. Noon found us becalmed and hungry; none of us had felt like eating for two days. We opened cans of soup and made stacks of sandwiches. T-bone steaks couldn't have tasted better. After gorging ourselves, we cleaned the boat, then spent the rest of the afternoon swimming in a glassy Atlantic.

It was a beautiful evening, but with no breeze we weren't going anywhere, unless we motored. The engine was wet and wouldn't start. I worked on it for an hour before it fired. Once it did, goodbye Gulf Stream. At dawn we broke through the radio blackout and fixed our position. We made our landfall around 10 P.M. and four hours later tied up in St. Augustine, Florida.

We were a ratty-looking bunch, all of us needing showers and clean clothes. After spreading half the boat's stores on the dock to dry out, we sought out a laundromat, found a shower at the gas dock; then, looking more like tourists than the old salts we were, we invaded a restaurant and ate everything on the menu. The following morning we were slow-boating once more down the Intercoastal Waterway.

Except for going aground one night—a not uncommon occurence in narrow parts of the channel—the next five days were uneventful but pleasant. As we motored past Stan's, a restaurant on the waterway in Fort Lauderdale, my old friend Audrey Arbuckles hailed us. I swung around, tied up, and in five minutes was having a cold beer with her. Buckles arranged the use of an apartment right on the waterway. We stayed there a week, Kyle spending most of it in the pool with the Avon rubber boat I had bought as *Molly Brown*'s dinghy.

It was a busy week. I had the compass and radio telephone repaired, the radio direction finder checked, and a rain catch and new hatch boards made. Robert and

John

Howard did the varnish work on *Molly Brown*. At this point, we had a change of crew. Bill Addison flew home to start a summer job, and John Tucker with a thousand pounds of baggage blew in.

I had met John while outfitting *Molly Brown* in Annapolis. He told me he wanted to go to Australia and make his fortune, then return to the U.S. and retire. I could understand that; I would like to have done the same thing myself. But what interested me most about John was his navigational training, skills acquired, he told me, while in a Naval Reserve unit. With his navy know-how and my correspondence course savvy, maybe together we could find our way to Australia. But before we got underway, I told him he would have to ship some of his stuff back home; he had brought more clothes than the rest of us combined. I sent some things home also, reducing my wardrobe to little more than a couple of pairs of jeans and several T-shirts.

We motored to Miami, then sailed down the Keys, fishing and snorkeling on the way. Not once did we get lost. With the channel marked the entire distance to Key West, the sextant became the most useless piece of equipment on board. At dusk on June 29, we sailed into a flotilla of black-boomed trawlers leaving Key West. They were shrimp boats, I learned later, making their regular nocturnal pilgrimage to net the night-feeding pink shrimp.

We tied up and walked over to Sloppy Joe's. An open-air bar frequented by assorted characters, it is reputed to have been Hemingway's hangout. For the next three days it became ours.

It was there I met Jack, a short, thin fellow in his forties. He wore a rumpled felt hat and reeked of gin. He was an old bomber pilot, World War II vintage. Buy him drinks and he'll tell war stories as long as there is something in his glass. I bought Jack drinks, and he obliged by not only entertaining me and my crew with yarns, he chauffered us around in his 1946 Chevrolet coupe as well. He drove me out to the airport to put Kyle on a plane, which was a tough thing for me to do. After being with her for three weeks, I wouldn't see her again for a year or more. For the first time since this wild-eyed project began, I began to have a few second thoughts. Perhaps Bill Addison was right. Maybe I was running away. Maybe I wouldn't make it back. Kyle, her cheeks wet, turned and waved. I watched the jet taxi out to the runway, then walked back to find Jack. He was at the National Airlines ticket counter banging his fist down and demanding a double gin on the rocks. The ticket girl informed him that the bar was at the other end of the airport. I accompanied him there and had a double myself.

I planned to sail that evening, but the engine wouldn't start. The trouble was a cracked distributor cap, which I set out to replace before all the stores closed. I found a new one, and I also found something else, something I had been intending to buy but kept forgetting. In a stationery shop window I saw a thick record book with a green, cloth-bound cover. I thought it would do and bought it. When I returned to the boat, I took a ball point pen and lettered on the cover: Log of Molly Brown.

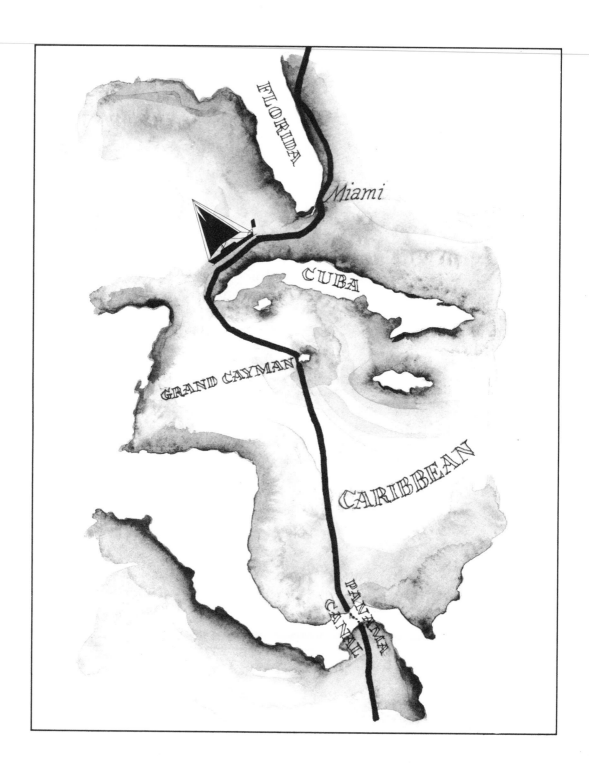

Chapter 1

Wednesday,
July 2, 1969:

We leave Key West at 0900 under clear skies and with a fresh easterly. I set a course for Isla Mujeres, on the western tip of the Yucatan Peninsula. At 1230 we hoist our candy-striped spinnacker. My crew is willing but inexperienced, has a tendency to let the boom jibe—slam to the other side. Speed is a steady five knots, course more southerly than I intended. We drop the spinnaker at 2200 and go on the main and headsail. For what it's worth, I got two fixes today with the sextant.

Thursday,
July 3:

I awaken at 0600 and immediately go into a state of shock. The mountains of Cuba loom off our port side. We made far more southing during the night than is healthy. I expect to see a gunboat any minute. We jibe and get back into the Gulf Stream. Our easterly fades, and we have to motor most of the night, wasting precious gas.

Friday,
July 4:

At dawn I decide to head back toward shore, where the current is more favorable. By mid-afternoon we leave the western tip of Cuba, three miles off our port side. The wind freshens again out of the east, and I decide to take advantage of it. Scratch Isla Mujeres.

Aim instead for Grand Cayman, some 300 miles away. Dark clouds build to the south. In the evening I try to establish radio contact with passing merchants in Yucatan Straits. No luck. I do raise a yacht that's lost, and give them position.

Sunday, July 6: The wind shifts to the southeast, right on *Molly Brown*'s nose. At 1400 we bang into a squall. *Molly Brown* is a pounder. She sails up on a wave, then falls over the crest with a crash that shakes the entire boat. If anybody's hungry, forget it.

Monday, July 7: We're beating into a 35-knot wind and bucking heavy seas. We have run out of fresh water, are not sure of our position, and the battery is dead. I consider bearing off to the Swan Islands. At sunset the Carribean takes pity; wind moderates and seas flatten. We motor toward Grand Cayman, spotting a flashing red beacon at 2300. We are 30 miles out of Georgetown.

Tuesday, July 8: We drop the hook in Georgetown Anchorage at 0200. Fifteen minutes later we are boarded by three drunks claiming to be customs officials. They demand to see our papers. I ask to see theirs first. They say they don't need papers, insist on seeing ours or it will cost us. In Yankee dollars, no doubt. I go below, load my shotgun, then come back up and order them off or I'll blast them off. They jump in their little rowboat and start paddling. I've never seen a rowboat move so quickly. They're gone, but their odor, that of sour rum, lingers. We sleep late—until a blast from the horn of a motor launch awakens us. Official-looking customs officials come aboard, examine our papers, and tell us where to anchor *Molly Brown*.

Sometimes I kept the log while ashore, sometimes I didn't. The latter was the case on Grand Cayman, but that's no problem. We were there only three days, and I remember everything that happened, which was very little. Halfway up the western arm of the island, near Georgetown—and across the sound from Rum Point—we signed in at the Pan Cayman House, specializing in american cuisine and booze. The owner said it was okay to anchor *Molly Brown* in front of the place, which was convenient for us and pleasing, I think, to him. This being the off-season for tourists—but not hurricanes—there weren't too many boats around, so *Molly Brown* stood out well. From the beach, I took color pictures of her, a practice I would repeat several thousand times during the voyage.

After dinner at the hotel, Robert, Howard, and John rounded up dates and went calypsoing. I stayed at the bar. There was one other American there—a dentist. He didn't say much, and neither did I. Conversation interferes with serious drinking.

The next morning we swam in the bluest water and sunned on the whitest beach in the world. That afternoon we went sightseeing in a rented English Ford. Two things particularly impressed me: a large tanker and a rusty cargo ship. They lay wrecked on a reef off the southern tip of the island. "That must have been one hell of a storm to have driven those ships aground," I remarked to the fellow who ran a restaurant nearby. That wasn't the cause of it at all, he told me. One ship was run on the reef to collect the insurance, the other by a drunken crew on a flat sea last Christmas Eve.

Refreshed, we sailed the following day a little before sundown. We had replenished our water cans, filled our jerry jugs with gasoline, and taken on enough fresh fruit to last a month. It shouldn't take that long, obviously, for us to reach the Panama Canal, 600 miles south. But don't bet on it; with our luck, we're apt to round the Horn and hit it from the Pacific side.

Friday, July 11:
With a fresh breeze out of the east at force five—about 25 knots—the taffrail log is spinning out

27

the miles. At 1500 a squall comes out of nowhere and clobbers us. Before we can get the jib down, the clew rips out; then the batten pockets in the mainsail tear.

Saturday, July 12:

It's still blowing and we're still going, but *Molly Brown* is as wet inside as out. The forward hatch is leaking, soaking clothes, bedding, and stores—the log included.

Sunday, July 13:

The day dawns clear, and we still have our breeze. I start the engine to charge the batteries. I add up the numbers and see that we have made almost 600 miles in four days. I never dreamed *Molly Brown* could go like that.

Monday, July 14:

Midmorning we sight the Panama coast, but where's the canal? I can't find it on a chart, because I forgot to get one of the Canal Zone. Luck is with us. We see a workman repairing a light on a marker, sail up close, ask him which way to the canal entrance. He points. As we motor toward the entrance, we treat ourselves to showers, a practice permitted only when near a port, where we can replenish our water supply. Soon after, we get another bath, thanks to suddenly falling rain. At 1400 we enter the canal. A launch lettered PCA—for Panama Canal Authority—comes alongside, and a uniformed official steps aboard to direct us to quarantine anchorage.

First, a misconception: I thought the Panama Canal runs east and west; actually, it's more north-south. Before the day was over I was running all four directions and getting no place. The reason was that the jolly, fat customs lady in Grand Cayman had cleared us for the Panamanian port Colón instead of where we were—and wanted to be—the American port Cristobal. That meant, the boarding officer told me, that we would have to go to Colón, three miles back, and clear in and clear out before we could clear in at Cristobal.

We motored to a busy dock at Colón and tied

up alongside a coaster unloading wheat. I looked up to see Panamanian National Guardsmen with carbines slung over their shoulders and pistols on their hips. Panama at that time was trying to decide who should run the country, and the fellows with the guns were insuring a fair outcome. In this trigger-happy atmosphere, I spent most of the afternoon running to customs, immigration, and police to clear in and, immediately afterwards, out. Without the aid of my taxi driver, I might have been there all night. He drove me from office to office, doubling as my interpreter. A big man with a big voice, he could easily out-shout—and, I'm confident, out-fight if need be—any procrastinating official. Finally, after paying port charges and the driver, I was back on *Molly Brown*. The guardsmen eyed her longingly as we left, wondering, perhaps, how long it would take to sink a fiberglass boat with carbines.

We motored back to Cristobal, hoisted our quarantine flag, and waited for PCA to clear us in. Two hours later no one had showed up, so we pumped up the Avon and went ashore uncleared. By 8 P.M. we were dining in the Cristobal Yacht Club, where mixed drinks cost 25 cents apiece. I drank a dollar's worth.

Connie

The next day Connie arrived. I had called her in Key West and persuaded her to meet me in Panama. Perhaps she would change her mind and sail across the Pacific with me. Wearing slacks and a bare midriff, she showed up at the yacht club in the afternoon, after a train ride across the isthmus. She looked great. To celebrate her arrival, the crew of *Molly Brown* partied throughout the night. At about 4 A.M., I hazily remember, John was still on the veranda of the yacht club trying to dance with a juke box.

We made it to *Molly Brown*, now in a slip, just several hours before our pilot came aboard. He was

Bob Farley—no relation to Luke, my former business associate. A husky, red-faced fellow in his forties, he was all business and, at least in the beginning, not very talkative. Piloting a yacht through the Panama Canal clearly didn't appeal to him. Yachts capsize, he complained; tow lines pull out deck fittings, and, referring to a recent experience, passengers sometimes complicate the day-long crossing by raising hell. While lunching on salami sandwiches, he told us a story of domestic strife that convinced Connie—if she had a notion—not to sail with me.

On the last yacht he piloted through the canal, Bob recounted, the man-and-wife crew fought and fussed the entire way. A few weeks later, he was summoned to testify in court. It seems that several hundred miles out of Panama, the man's wife suddenly developed appendicitis and died. Because the weather was hot, he buried her at sea. He returned to Balboa, a police inquiry was held, and after Bob and others who knew the couple testified, the case was closed. "Who can say for sure what happens at sea?" Bob said.

At dusk, *Molly Brown* nosed into a slip at the yacht club in Balboa, the American port on the Pacific end of the canal. Throughout the all-day, 50-mile trip, not a harsh word was heard on the boat, which I'm sure Bob Farley appreciated.

Before tackling the Pacific, I had to administer first-aid to *Molly Brown*. Her hatches leaked, salt water entered the fuel tank through the vent, and her topsides and deck were coated with oil from the dirty harbor in Cristobal. I also had to buy supplies, repair a camera, and acquire charts of the Pacific. When I left Key West, I assumed it would be easy to get the charts in the Canal Zone. I rented a car and looked all over Balboa. Not one chart did I find. Connie and I drove back across the isthmus to Cristobal, where we had better luck. A yachtsman there had left California bound for Australia but changed his mind in mid-ocean and headed for the British West Indies. I bought his charts for a dollar each and returned to Balboa in time to say goodbye to Robert and Howard. They were flying to Mexico City, from where they planned to hitchhike home.

John Tucker, meanwhile, was enjoying the local attractions, one of whom was a pretty Panamanian girl. She and John joined Connie and me aboard *Molly Brown*, and we motored to the sleepy island of Taboga, six miles from Balboa. We picnicked on sandwiches and a bottle of wine in the old courtyard while the villagers gawked. Not too many Americans get over there, evidently.

This is not to knock people-watching. I did it myself, usually in the yacht club bar in Balboa. In the afternoon, sailors from all parts of the world assembled there to have drinks and swap yarns. Being new at the game of ocean walloping, I thought I might learn something from these more experienced gentlemen. But no one can really tell you about the ocean. As a fellow from Australia said, "You have to sort it out for yourself."

I met some interesting people at the bar. There was Lester Ball, an Englishman of about 60, who had sailed across the Atlantic with his attractive, 26-year-old secretary, Yvonne. He had a nasty scar on his forehead, reminder of a fall on deck one night in rough weather. Yvonne had sewn up the gash and made Lester comfortable. It was Lester who put the idea in my head of going to the Galapagos Islands. "You would be silly to miss them," he said, and he proved to be right. We also would have missed Maryrose, whom you will meet soon.

One day a big, burly fellow with a long, red beard and sad eyes entered the bar. He looked like a

Viking, and he was, in a public-relations kind of way. Captain Duvall—I've forgotten his first name—was master of the 90-foot Danish schooner *Frie*. Leaving Denmark under full sail, the ship had set out for California on a promotional stunt with a cargo of Plumrose hams, Tuborg beer, and Avon dinghies. The success of the stunt depended upon the ship reaching its destination, and the prospects, according to Capt. Duvall, weren't good. His ship had come close to foundering in the Caribbean when her seams opened in heavy weather. A U.S. Coast Guard plane responded to his distress calls and dropped a pump. With that, his crew saved the vessel from sinking until it reached the canal, then deserted. The only way to keep the ship afloat, the captain concluded, was to eat the hams and drink the beer. Would we help him? Smiles beaming all around, we climbed into the rented car and drove to the dock where the ship was tied up.

The PCA had not permitted her to anchor in the harbor for fear she would sink and block traffic. I could not argue with that, nor with the crew's decision to abandon her. The *Frie* was a dirty, rotting old hulk that remained afloat only by force of habit. Capt. Duvall said she was 50 years old. I would have laid eight to five odds she was at least a hundred and even money that she would sink by morning. It was, therefore, an act of mercy that we lightened her cargo until we could drink no more.

Touring the Panamanian countryside was a pleasure, and Connie did most of the driving because her sense of direction was better than mine. She would have made a great navigator. One of the few times I took the wheel was in Panama City, and I regretted it the instant the Panamanian militiaman flagged us to the curb. I had violated some damned traffic regulation, and he demanded to see my passport. I produced it. He pocketed it, explaining that it would be returned when I appeared in court the following morning at eight o'clock. Then he handed me a ticket.

That complicated things. Connie was leaving the next morning—at about the time I was scheduled to be in court. But even if she wasn't, I didn't want to go to court. I don't like courts, domestic or foreign. For a second, I thought of trying to buy my passport back. Then I had a better idea, truly a flash of inspiration. I turned to the militiaman and said in a steely voice: "I am the captain of an American ship due to sail at midnight. If I am delayed, you are in big trouble, mister." He forked over the passport, saluted, and waved us on—Connie driving, of course.

That evening I took Connie to dinner at the Senorial, an excellent restaurant on the outskirts of Panama City. We had chateaubriand and Nuit St. George wine. I was to see a lot of the world before I would eat another chateaubriand and drink a bottle of Nuit St. George with Connie again.

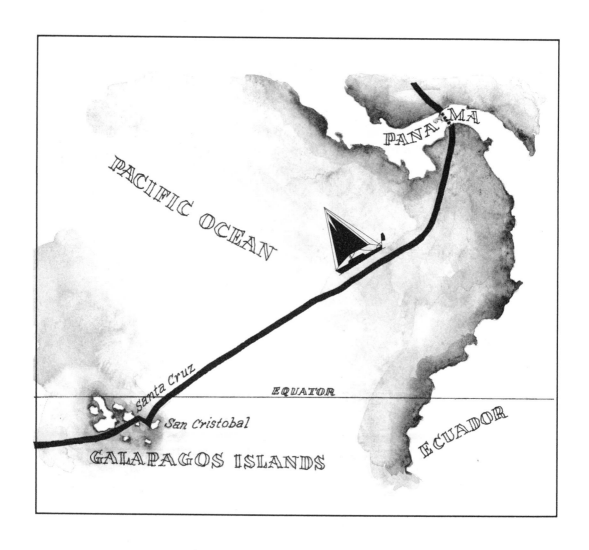

PANAMA

PACIFIC OCEAN

Santa Cruz

EQUATOR

San Cristobal

GALAPAGOS ISLANDS

ECUADOR

Chapter 2

Wednesday, July 30:	*Molly Brown* under power departs Balboa at 1345, which must be rush hour in the Gulf of Panama. Our course is southwest for the Galapagos, a 900-mile run. We log 50 of it in light winds.
Thursday, July 31:	Morning finds us in a dead calm; we resume motoring. I decide we will use our gas to get out of the doldrums and into the trades. It rains in the afternoon. I grab a bar of soap and we shower on deck. At 2200 John tries to call Lester on 2182 mc, but can't raise him. All we want to say is goodbye.
Sunday, August 3:	After two more days of fluky weather, we finally find some air. At 1100 we are beating into a force three breeze out of the southwest. We sight the Malpelo rocks in the afternoon and set a more westerly course. John is fishing. He fishes constantly. Not because he enjoys catching and eating fish, but because he hates and fears fish. He considers fish to be his natural enemy. He wants to catch and kill every fish in the Pacific Ocean. So far, he has lost a couple of lures and caught nothing.
Monday, August 4:	It's clear and windy, a perfect washday. We launder with water from the rain catch, then hang up

the clothes to dry. Undershorts ballon in the wind like small spinnakers. We overtake a large sea turtle, tack about for a closer look, but lose him. No turtle soup for dinner.

Tuesday, August 5: The sea is like a lake, and *Molly Brown* is skimming over it at five knots or better. About noon porpoises swim alongside and scare John half to death. He's afraid they are going to jump into the cockpit and attack us. The danger passes, though, and he goes back to fishing with a vengeance. The result: another lost lure. We're running low on fishing tackle.

Wednesday, August 6: *Molly Brown* is pounding and the gas tank is banging, knocking the bunks loose in the foreward cabin. We should have tied down the tank in Balboa. More bad news: John has stopped up the head. He has been constipated since leaving Panama. This morning he took an Ex-lax, and it worked; but it was too much for the head. "You stopped it up," I tell him, "so you take it out and bring it up on the cockpit and unstop it." He takes it out, hands it to me, and I drop it. So now we have a broken, stopped-up head. Finally we get it unstopped, and I fiberglass it together. (Note: It held until I got back to Annapolis—more than a year later—then shattered like an egg when I dropped a can of shaving cream in it.)

Friday, August 8: Today is like yesterday—cloudy and depressing. We're plowing into force four winds, and the gas tank is banging again. Why did Jim Mercereau install it in the forepeak? A noon sun shot fails, so at twilight I try for a celestial fix and get it.

Saturday, August 9: With clearing skies, I get a morning fix. We are 150 miles north of our dead-reckoning position. Taking a more southerly tack, we make landfall at 1400. We have zigzagged 1100 miles in 11 days. This close to land John and I stand four-hour watches. I figure we crossed the equator about midnight.

Tired of tacking, we switch to motor power at 1100 for the 40 remaining miles to Bahia Wreck, the harbor of San Cristóbal Island. Several hours later John finally hooks a fish—a 28-inch dolphin—which we have for dinner. At 1930 *Molly Brown* is swinging at anchor, and John and I, with a fifth of Johnny Walker, are sitting on the cabin top drinking in the sights. A patrol boat brings the Ecuadorian port officer. He takes our papers and passports, tells us we can come ashore in the morning, then bids us a friendly *buenas noches.*

After being confined to the cramped quarters of a small boat for two weeks, we were eager to step on land and see if we still remembered how to walk. The opposite is also true: A few days ashore and we were ready for another balancing act aboard *Molly Brown.* The port officer returned our passports and within seconds we had the Avon in the water and were paddling for a quay that jutted into the harbor. To someone used to shiny chrome, neon lights, and polluted air, the scene before us was a throwback to pioneer days. A row of wooden houses with rusty tin roofs fronted the beach; if a ragged Robinson Crusoe had stepped out of one, I wouldn't have been surprised. Tied to the quay were several small fishing boats. I noticed a few dogs, a goat on a leash, and two donkeys sound asleep on their feet. Not one automobile did I see. There was a restaurant, however—Ruth's—the only one on the island. As you might expect, it didn't have a menu; you ate what happened to be in the pot, typically goat or fresh pork and typically good. It was served with rice and mugs of warm beer. Rum was also available.

We lunched at Ruth's with Senōr Garcia, the immigration officer. Afterwards we walked to his home to get our passports stamped. In setting the dial on his stamp, Senōr Garcia made a mistake and gave us visas for ten years instead of ten days. Mine is good until November 11, 1979.

Taking Senõr Garcia's advice, we decided to visit the village of El Progresso high on the flank of a volcano—inactive, the Senõr assured us. All the Galapagos were formed by volcanoes, and some of the islands are as barren as moonscapes. San Cristóbal, however, is green and fertile, and the higher you go the greener it becomes. We piled into an ancient flatbed truck, squeezing in among El Progresso villagers returning home with their dogs and chickens. The road was winding and rutted and, at steep grades, proved to be more than the old truck could pull without lightening its cargo. We would get off and walk while the truck labored in low gear up to a more gentle incline. Then everyone would get back on and, continuing nonstop conversations, immediately raise their voices in efforts to be heard above the roar of the motor. It was during this ride that John screwed up his courage and tried to speak Spanish with the islanders. But it was a bust. They couldn't understand him. Made John madder than hell. "I don't know what's wrong with these people," he said.

El Progresso was backward but beautiful. It had no electricity or plumbing, and the villagers drew water from a single well. The view from the heights, however, more than made up for the lack of mainland creature comforts. I was content just to stand and gaze and feel sorry for my friends in Maryland who would never see the equal of this if they lived for a thousand years and made a trillion dollars. Beside every little wooden house was a lush vegetable garden, and orange trees with the sweetest fruit I have ever tasted grew wild. Donkeys loved them. They would lie under the trees and eat oranges all day without bothering to spit out the seeds. Here was a true garden of Eden, and not only for jackasses.

There was a little one-room school in El Progresso named Carlos Darwin, after the British naturalist who came to the Galapagos in 1835 and spent a few weeks studying the wildlife. Charles Darwin was about the hottest thing ever to hit the Galapagos, for it was here that he began pondering his famous theory of evolution. He pondered for 24 years, then wrote a book called *The Origin of the Species*, which I've heard about but haven't read. I later met an Englishman who had, and he said it was bunk that man descended from apes. "Apes have always been apes and that's all they ever will be," he said. We drank a bottle of whiskey and let it go at that.

Since the truck wasn't returning to Bahia Wreck until morning, John and I walked back down the lava trail enjoying the magnificent scenery and helping ourselves to the oranges. Coming down, we saw that two yachts had sailed into the harbor while we were sightseeing. On one of them, *Bronzewing,* a handsome boat of about 45 feet, we dined that evening as guests of Julian Fitter.

Julian, tall and blond and bronzed by the sun, was the son-in-law of Carl Angermeyer, resident of the Galapagos since the late thirties, when he fled Hitler's Germany. He knows more about the islands than anybody, Julian told me, and I've never heard it disputed. Julian bought *Bronzewing* in England and sailed her across the Atlantic and through the Panama Canal to the Galapagos, where he planned to charter her to tourists. With him came a young couple who, as I soon learned, were Jehovah's Witnesses. Surmising that I could use a little religion, they asked me after dinner if I would like to see their literature. I politely declined, explaining that taking up a religion was to me like buying a car. Once you decided you needed one, it really didn't make a hell of a lot of difference what kind you chose. I was not in a buying mood.

Conversation was more relaxed with Julian's guests from the other yacht I had seen. Bob and Marie Grant told me they had left New Zealand ten years ago. Home became wherever they dropped anchor, and that took in a lot of territory—from the South Pacific to the West Indies. They were the first "yachties" I met. A yachty, as it was explained to me later in Australia—where the term originated, I suspect—is a vagabond sailor who lives by his wits. He's a hippy of the high seas who bums around in a sailboat, usually one he's knocked together himself, and he will stay in a port until he scrapes up enough money to make another passage. Sometimes port authorities ask him to leave before he is ready, but that, I suppose, is part of the price you pay for not having to pay income taxes. In this context, I hasten to add I was not a yachty nor did I intend to become one; but, of course, I'm over 30. Bob and Marie and their son, Guy, had been in the Galapagos for two months. How much longer they stayed, I don't know, perhaps indefinitely. One thing's for sure: They wouldn't have starved; that is, if they liked oranges.

For the next couple of days John and I divided our time between Ruth's and *Molly Brown*—the former for refreshment, the latter out of necessity. While John mended the mainsail, I worked on our clattering gas tank—which reminded me that we needed gas. Since there were no service stations within a thousand miles, finding it presented a problem. My best bet, I reasoned, was the naval installation on San Cristóbal. It was a bad bet. Diesel fuel? *Si.* Gasoline? No. Sailing across the Pacific without a cupful of gas in the tank didn't appeal to me, so I went back to Ruth's to think some more. A dollop of rum cleared my head. The truck! It burned gas. The revelation was staggering. All I needed to do was tap the truck's source. And that, I found out, was Carlos Darwin Catholic School, which boasted a gasoline generator. John and I went up the hill with empty jerry jugs and came down again with 20 gallons strapped to a donkey full of orange juice. We paid 60 cents a gallon and counted our blessings.

From the navy we got water and a $23.23 clearing bill. We bought rum for a dollar a gallon and a hundred-pound sack of oranges for fifty cents. We stocked up on vegetables at comparable prices, except for avocados. Senõr Garcia gave us a whole basketful of them. At noon Thursday, the fourteenth of August, we weighed anchor and set sail for the tiny island of Sante Fe, also known as Barrington.

We arrived at dusk, just in time for John to catch a fish for dinner. The next morning we went ashore in the Avon and were greeted by a reception committee of several hundred barking sea lions. They and iguanas, finches, wild goats, and other Darwinian creatures are the sole inhabitants of this barren rock. The sea lions let us get close enough to pet them, but the goats kept at a respectable distance. Not that we wanted to pet them; I wanted to shoot one to replenish our fresh meat inventory. Failing that, I laid down my shotgun and loaded my camera. For the next couple of hours I scrambled over the rocks exposing color film. Considering the pleasure I have since derived from my pictures, I came out way ahead that day—and the goats sure as hell did.

By mid-afternoon John and I were back on *Molly Brown* and heading west for Santa Cruz, about a four-hour sail. The sinking sun silhouetted the island, a massive cone of lava with its tip broken off. By the time we had anchored in Academy Bay and found our way to Forest Nelson's hotel—actually a dining room and bar with a string of small cottages—the dinner hour was over. At least that's what we were told at the bar. John and I were resigned to returning to *Molly*

Brown and opening up a can of something when a tall, full-breasted girl with big brown eyes entered the room. Speaking with authority gloved in a French accent, she said there was plenty of food in the kitchen and saw no reason why we couldn't be served. That woke up the place and started things stirring in the kitchen.

Maryrose

I told the girl I appreciated her bending the rules and invited her to have a drink with us. She was, I assumed from her outspokenness, managing the place. No, she said, Forest Nelson had hired her as a tourist guide, but there were few tourists. As for speaking up in our behalf, that was just her way. She didn't stand on convention and couldn't abide people who did. Her name was Maryrose Monnier and she was 24. I liked her.

The following evening I had dinner with Maryrose, then escorted her home, to one of the cottages. I poured us a drink and told her what my plans were. She told me she had none, and kicked off her shoes. She had left her native Switzerland five years before, worked her way through Canada, California, Brazil, finally landing in the Galapagos six months ago. She would have liked to return to the United States, but aside from finding transportation, there was the problem of securing a work permit. Although I would hear variations on her story later, at best it was a sticky situation.

As for my situation, I was with each passing day more strongly committed to a circumnavigation. John was not, Australia being his destination, which, as it happened, he fell short of by several thousand miles. I hadn't given much thought to what I would do about a crew when John left, but now I did. A crew member who could cook and keep the boat tidy and me contented seemed an adequate replacement for one who fished day and night. I kicked off my shoes and asked Maryrose if she had ever been on a sailboat. She yawned and said no. I asked her if she would like to try it. She said yes. With the understanding that I would take her as far as Tahiti, I told her to be on the dock ready to go at eight in the morning. When I left her, at about midnight, she was feeling pretty good. I didn't feel badly myself.

The distance from the Galapagos to the Marquesas Islands is about 3300 miles, with nothing in between but a lot of nothing. As I stood on the dock Sunday morning waiting for Maryrose, I looked out onto that big blue waterbed and tried to comprehend its vastness from here to there, in terms I could grasp. The best I could come up with was that it would be like crossing the United States in a covered wagon without stopping at a single saloon the entire way. It might take *Molly Brown* a month or more to cover such a distance, maybe less. A lot depended upon how lucky we were: whether or not we escaped sickness, fire, or, as John feared, a fish attack. The threat of mutiny I didn't consider. Running out of water I did. Fifty gallons is not a lot; I've used that much in a weekend on Chesapeake Bay. Running out of food was less a possibility, though it could happen if we got lost—of which we were capable—and if the fish quit biting. *Molly Brown*, despite her bone-shaking pounding, didn't worry me. But if disaster did hit us, I thought, swinging my gaze back to the solid lump of Santa Cruz, there wasn't a damned thing we could do about it. Out in the middle of the Pacific chances were slight that a distress call would be heard or a flare seen. Maryrose, fresh as the morning in a red print shift and with her dark hair tied back, walked up to the dock and, without a trace of anxiety, tossed her bag onto the boat. "Did you think I wasn't coming?" she said.

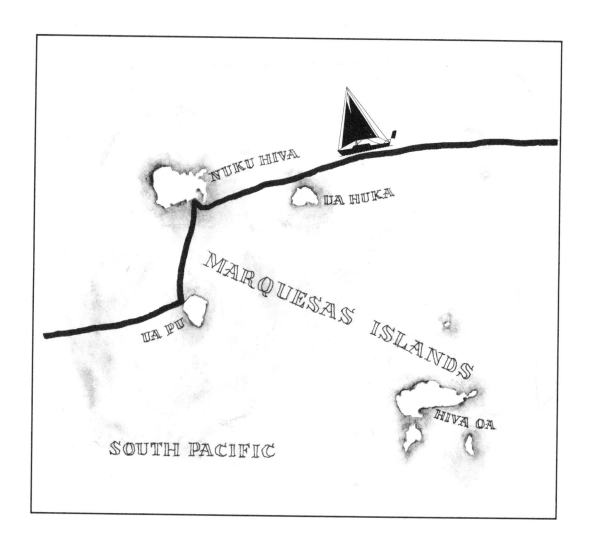

Chapter 3

Sunday,
August 17:

We sail at 1330 under clear skies. Winds are light and variable. At 1430 John discovers he has crabs. He bought a blanket in San Cristobal, and the little fellows must have come with it. I close up the cabin tight and spray it with a can of insecticide. The label says it's effective against roaches, fleas, mosquitoes, silverfish, and crickets. Doesn't mention crabs. I spray anyway, with particular attention to John's blanket and John himself. Maryrose gets upchucking sick, either from the spray or the rolling sea or both, and is unable to cook dinner. I open a can of tuna, a can of peas, a can of corn, a can of mushroom soup; mix them together, heat them, serve them. There are no spoken complaints.

Monday,
August 18:

We sleep till 0900. There is no sea and the winds are force two. I set the spinnaker at noon. John is still at war with the crabs. Maryrose is still seasick. By popular demand I do not fix dinner. We snack on oranges, avocados, bread.

Tuesday,
August 19:

Beautiful day. John's crabs are gone. He credits it to the can of powder he found in the medicine locker. The only can of powder in there that I know of is foot powder. Maryrose also seems okay, which means we're eating better. Her dinner menu: tossed salad, french fries, barbecued chicken. With a clear horizon at twilight, I shoot four stars and two planets. We are 300 miles out and moving—at seven knots the last four hours.

Wednesday, August 20:

At 0930 I set the spinnaker and staysail, which is just what *Molly Brown* ordered. From fix to fix she makes a good 130 miles. I write letters. One to Connie begins, "Everything is going so well, it is scary." Tonight I sit on deck for a long time and watch the stars and let my thoughts ramble. John, as usual, is trailing two lines. Maryrose is asleep. At 2300 I check the self-steerer, open the hatches, switch off all lights, and crawl into my bunk. John is already asleep, but he's still fishing. A line leading down through the companionway is tied to his ankle. I'm a bit dubious about this alarm system. If a half-ton tuna strikes, he could go hurtling out of the cabin into the ocean. I lie there wondering if I should awaken John and warn him of the danger. On second thought, I think I'll sleep on it.

Thursday, August 21:

I arise at 1000 and breakfast on curried eggs and toast. John, I'm relieved to learn, survived the night; he didn't get a strike. I leave Maryrose reading *Kon-Tiki* and take my coffee on deck. I tell John of my concern for his safety, and he promises not to tie the line to his ankle. He will tie it to his wrist. The wind freshens in the afternoon to force four and we drop the spinnaker. Great sailing.

Friday, August 22:

During the night flying fish bombard the boat, and they are all over the deck. I pick up a bunch of them, clean them, give them to Maryrose to fry for breakfast. Delicious. The fish can't see us coming at night and blindly jump aboard. Some of them damn near land in the skillet. I spend much of the day on the cabin top bird-watching. Storm petrels dart among the waves, then alight on the water and start walking on it. I understand they are clumsy on land. At 1830 I fix our position at 3°23' south latitude, 102°10' west longitude. We are dead on course and riding easy at six knots.

Saturday, August 23: Beautiful day with the wind backing toward the east. Disaster in the afternoon: I have crabs. The little sons of bitches got tired of eating on John and are now chewing on me. All we can do is spray and pray. John used all the foot powder.

Sunday, August 24: I awaken early to bathe and shampoo, then rub on mosquito repellent in hopes it will repell crawling things. After lunch I shoot the sun. After dinner Maryrose catches a fish, but this is no ordinary fish. She hauls in a snake mackerel. We know it's a snake mackerel because there is a photograph of one just like it in *Kon-Tiki.* Thor Heyerdahl says the fish lives at great depths and that his crew caught the only one ever landed on a line. I would have liked to mount the second one ever caught on a line and bring it home to hang over the mantel. Instead, we decide to have it for breakfast.

Monday, August 25: The snake mackerel is tasty. We finish off the last of our San Cristóbal bread, and none too soon. It was getting stale. Our Balboa eggs are keeping well. A celestial fix at 1900 shows us to be almost 1300 miles out of the Galapagos. I take the radio on deck and pick up "Voice of America." After hearing the latest on Viet Nam, pollution, and other goodies from civilization, I turn the damn thing off and get a book— *Hurricane Years,* by Cameron Hawley.

Tuesday, August 26: Today is my birthday, and there's not a candle on the boat. Instead of birthday cake we have birthday daiquiris prepared by John. Cheers. After dinner— ham-and-rice casserole—we sip green creme de menthe. Only one flaw mars an otherwise perfect day: No. 1 genoa has to come down because it's been chafed through by the pulpit. We hoist No. 2 genny and drop the main for the night. Wind is due east at force five, and *Molly Brown* is charging.

Wednesday, August 27: Overcast. We set twin headsails—not a bad combination. Less yawing, though we sacrifice some speed. Excitement at 2000. Lights from a passing ship loom far off our port bow then quickly fade. Must be a tramp or fishing trawler since there are no shipping lanes in this part of the Pacific. In two weeks this has been the only evidence we have seen that other people are sharing the ocean. It is either comforting or depressing, I don't know which.

Friday, August 29: Yesterday was clear sailing, and so is today.

Saturday, August 30: Good breakfast of flying fish, rice, eggs, and saltines. Maryrose is a damned good cook, lots of imagination. She laced the scrambled eggs with a dash of Worcestershire sauce, a nice touch, especially for eggs as old as these are. At 1900 I shoot the stars and do some adding and subtracting. We are 2005 miles out, and *Molly Brown* is charging across the Pacific like a runaway horse.

Sunday, August 31: Wind has backed to northeast and is blowing up pretty strong. Seas have built up so much that the self-steerer can't prevent *Molly Brown* from yawing, which causes the main to jibe and me to cuss. I drop the main and attempt to set twin headsails, but there's too much wind. Back up goes the main and No. 2 genny on a starboard tack. In the evening the wind honks up and I take down the main and go with the genny. I've got blisters on my hands, and John probably has them too—on his butt. He's been sitting all day fishing.

Monday, September 1: We averaged less than five knots through the night. I set the drifter and No. 1 genoa to see what happens. It is a good guess; speed increases to almost six knots. After dinner I finish *Hurricane Years*.

Tuesday, September 2:	It's a fine morning, warm and sunny; but my disposition isn't. The servo blade on the self-steerer breaks, the drifter tears, and a winch handle falls into the ocean. John makes a new blade with fenderboard, but it's too short to get enough purchase in the water. I'm not worried. We have only about 650 miles to go, and John and I can steer *Molly Brown* that far. John takes the first watch. When I come up to relieve him at midnight, I find him standing backwards in the cockpit, facing the stern of the boat. I ask him if he doesn't think it's better to turn around and steer the boat properly. He says no, he likes the feel of the wind in his face. I do not say what I feel like saying and begin my watch with the wind at my back.
Wednesday, September 3:	I glue the blade together with epoxy and let it dry. Tomorrow I'll put it in the water and see if it holds. Maryrose steers while John sleeps and I work on running lights, which have decided not to work. Barometer is falling. By mid-afternoon the weather turns squally. After dark it's blown up quite a bit, and I ask John to go up on the foredeck and take down one of the headsails. Since I've made most of the sail changes thus far, I don't feel badly about asking him. He takes down the sail, but not very willingly. Maybe he thinks it will cost him a strike while away from his fishing lines.
Thursday, September 4:	During my watch—1200 to 0400—I check on deck and discover that John left the spinnaker pole extended from the mast. At breakfast I ask him why he hadn't taken the pole down when he changed the sail. He replies that he had done half the job and that I could do the other half. John is good company in port, but at sea he is as useless as balls on a priest. At noon I put the servo blade in the water, while we are becalmed. At 1445 we get a little light air and the damned thing breaks again. I pull it out and do what should have been done in the first place: through-bolt

it to a section of fenderboard. The splice works, even if it doesn't look pretty. With the Hasler back in business, everybody sleeps tonight.

Friday, September 6: We made only 50 miles during the night, and we're still crawling. I change course, opting for a little more southing, then get to work on those damned lights again. Tonight a fresh breeze honks up out of the east. We're on the move once more.

Sunday, September 7: Clear, sunny day with a steady, force four easterly. A sun line at 0915 puts us 210 miles out of Nuku Hiva in the Marquesas. At 1900 I shoot five stars and compute we are 150 miles out. We drop double headsails and go with the No. 1 genny and main. John caps a perfect day by boating a nice dolphin.

Monday, September 8: Landfall at 0830. Ua Huka, east of Nuku Hiva, is sitting right where the chart says it should. Since it's no more than a pinpoint on a wall map, I'm astounded we found it so easily. The Marquesas are step two islands, which means they rise right up from the ocean floor; there are few coral reefs or shoal areas around them. A small vessel like *Molly Brown* can sail up close and still have a hundred fathoms of water under her. We skirt the island and bear westward for Nuku Hiva, which comes into view at 1430. Four hours later we round Cape Martin and see a cluster of tall peaks topped with clouds that look like globs of whipped cream. We scan for two large rocks that my sailing directions identify as the entrance to the bay where we can anchor. As night falls, the island looms before us as a black, massive wall. We drop sail and cautiously motor alongside it, feeling our way in the darkness. Suddenly I see a rock dead ahead and swing out around it. Behind it appear lights. We head toward them like a moth to a flame. At 2230 we drop anchor in still water. It took us only 22 days to make the passage—an average of 150 miles a day.

A log can be deceptive. For Tuesday,

September 9, mine reads: "We arise 0830, have fried fish for breakfast. The bay is beautiful." A lot of places are beautiful, but what awed us this morning was something to behold. The water, a richer, deeper blue than the pure blue sky, lapped softly against a crescent of dazzling white sand fringed with palm trees and thatched houses. Behind them and high above them, needle-peaked mountains hung in velvety green folds like a vast curtain about to open. Beautiful? We had found, after three weeks of seemingly aimless sailing, a piece of paradise. I was anxious to go ashore.

There were numerous small fishing boats in the bay and one other yacht, the handsome yawl *Eleuthera,* an apt name in this setting. We rowed over in the Avon and introduced ourselves to Earl and Paula Shank, a pleasant couple in their fifties from Seattle. Earl briefed us on the island—where to find the port authority, get supplies, have our clothes laundered. We accepted the Shanks offer to have drinks with them that evening on the boat, then returned to *Molly Brown* for showers.

Clean but a little rumpled, we made for shore. Most of the activity was centered around the new quay being built for the trade schooner that called once a month. Except for a wayfaring yacht like ours, the schooner is about the only contact the islanders have with the outside world. There is no airfield in the Marquesas. We beached the dinghy and headed up the dirt road that rimmed a small village. Low neat houses roofed with palm thatch fronted the bay. Windows that were never shuttered opened into sparsely furnished rooms with wooden floors. Straw mats served as beds. If the houses were modest, the yards were not. Banks of orchids and flowering shrubs framed emerald lawns. Frangipani and hibiscus trees were in full flower, and some of the women wore the blossoms in their hair.

The Polynesians are, in my estimation, the truly beautiful people. Amber-skinned, dark-eyed, black-haired, they have attractive features and carefree ways. The men tend to be tall and well-proportioned, the women heavy-bosomed and plump. All go barefoot, and many wear floppy straw hats. As we passed them, they smiled, some of them greeting us in French. I thought I had never met a friendlier people or been made to feel so welcome.

We came to the gendarme's house, where Earl Shank had told us we would be issued visas. A tall, rotund man—he must have weighed 270 pounds—the gendarme seemed pleasant and accommodating. He prepared our visas while conversing with Maryrose in French. What happened next shattered the tranquility of the island. He and Maryrose began shouting at each other. I don't know who started the argument, or what it was all about, but I suspect Maryrose dropped the first insult. She could be damned feisty at times. The result was that John and I received visas and she didn't.

On the way back to *Molly Brown* we stopped in at Maurice's, a little store crammed with barrels of rice, potatoes, onions, and other items. Earl Shank was having a cold beer at the bar, a tiny room that opened into the store. It was a bar because Maurice, who was old and thin and Chinese, had a refrigerator there in which he kept beer. It was also a restaurant because you could buy goose liver Pâté and crackers in the store and bring them to the little room to have with your drink. After we lunched with Earl, he pointed out the baker's shop and the public shower. Regaining her cool, Maryrose decided to make another try for her visa. I headed for the shower. John agreed to seek out the lady who did laundry.

By nightfall we were all back on *Molly Brown*,

John with our laundered clothes, Maryrose with her visa, and super-clean me. I'd had a third shower. Two things I miss at sea are cold beer and hot showers, and when I come ashore, I try to correct those deficiencies as quickly as possible.

We spent the evening on Earl's boat drinking his Scotch and listening to his life story. He had made a lot of money manufacturing surgical equipment, enough at least to quit the rat race. He and Paula sailed to the Marquesas to retire and, he emphasized, to help the Polynesians. While I hadn't been here long, I couldn't see that the Polynesians needed much help. It looked to me like they had things pretty much the way they wanted them. I was a little drunk when I got back to *Molly Brown*. But, what the hell, it had been awhile—a month, anyway.

Next morning we went ashore and met the French administrator of the islands. He must have charmed Maryrose, for she never made any ugly faces at him. Lunch was at Maurice's. He was the island's ships' chandler as well as its grocer, and showed us the log he kept of visiting yachts. The last entry caught my eye. The 42-foot yawl *La Salle,* crewed by Hal and Sally Autenreith and their four children, had sailed from Annapolis in November, 1968. Maurice asked if I knew them, and I replied that I didn't. There was a snapshot of the boat in the log, but I couldn't recall ever seeing *La Salle* in Annapolis. It had left the Marquesas a month ago bound for Tahiti, our destination.

Thursday was shopping day. While John scouted for fresh eggs, Maryrose and I went to Maurice's for canned goods, rice, coffee, and the like. He told us where we could buy fresh vegetables and, as there were no taxis on the island, we set out on foot. There was, in fact, only one automobile on Nuku Hiva—the administrator's. Our walk through the village led to an upland trail, which we decided to explore. Wending through palms and ferns, we came to a stream in which children were playing with little hand-carved boats. Their mothers, busy washing clothes on flat-topped boulders, smiled and hailed us in French. Thirst and fatigue overtook us farther up the trail, and we started down, pausing at the stream while Maryrose asked one of the washerwomen how to get to the vegetable seller Maurice recommended. An hour later we were standing beside an old Chinese man, his face wrinkled by years of toil lavished on his lush garden. He sold us lettuce, parsley, cabbages, potatoes, cucumbers, lemons, as much as we could carry. In a shed nearby, Polynesian craftsmen were making wood carvings—beautiful things. I bought a Tiki—or Sun God—for five dollars. I later regretted I did not get more, for I never again saw carvings so fine.

We returned to find *Molly Brown* anchored closer to shore. She had drug her 22-pound Danforth anchor during the morning and was drifting to sea. Fortunately, two Polynesian men noticed what was happening and raced out in a canoe with an outboard motor and brought her back. I vowed then not to be so damned careless about where I anchored. A fellow could lose his shirt—as well as his boat—by such negligence.

That evening the Shanks had dinner with us at a small restaurant on the island. The conversation was lively. I could not understand how anyone not born to it could spend the rest of his life in such a remote place, no matter how lovely. They could not fathom how anyone could enjoy banging around the world in a small boat. With such divergent views, it was strange that we should meet on the same little island, one of us here in quest of excitement and adventure, the other here for ease and relaxation. It really did not make much difference. The broiled fish was good, the wine drinkable, and the South Pacific night delightful. We strolled along the beach until we talked ourselves out, then went to our boats.

The less said about Friday the better. Nauseated, weak, aching, we lay in our bunks all day and thought about such things as last wills and testaments and extreme unction. Evidently that delicious fish we had eaten the night before was not grade A. I took some small comfort from our first-aid book, under the heading food poisoning. It said that if you didn't die in the first 24 hours, you would probably recover.

Saturday morning came, and I was still alive. In fact, I felt surprisingly good. John and Maryrose were also coming around, and about 10 A.M. they rolled out of their bunks. We washed, sipped some hot tea, then went ashore to collect our supplies and exchange goodbyes. We stopped at the little Catholic mission in the village, dropped something in the box, and continued on to Maurice's where we met Earl. He looked a mite pale. The tainted fish had also waylaid him and Paula. But he felt well enough to have a beer, and I always had one or two when in Maurice's whether I was thirsty or not. Next stop was the bakery, where we picked up bread, cookies, and a couple of cakes. Supplies stowed, water cans filled, we weighed anchor at high noon and made for the island of Ua Pu, 26 miles to the South. This would be our jumping-off point for Tahiti.

On the chart, little Ua Pu looks much like an arrowhead. Seen from sea level, it still looks like an arrowhead, one tapering to a point 4,000 feet high. We entered the harbor in late afternoon and dropped anchor near a trading ship that was unloading supplies into lighters. Some of the cargo must have been 100 proof, for the tall Polynesian gendarme who met us as we stepped ashore was drunk. Maryrose got going with him in French, and relationships began deteriorating rapidly. I coaxed her back into the rubber dinghy. I had half a notion to sail right then, but *Molly Brown* needed a scrubbing, which I decided to do first thing in the morning.

Not long after sunrise I was scouring the topsides with Ajax. It was hot work, but the boat looked a lot better for it. I was in the water working on her bottom when the gendarme, sober and cheerful, arrived in an outrigger canoe. He was in a trading mood. With Maryrose interpreting, he asked if I had any .22 rifle cartridges. I scurried below and came up with my 16-gauge shotgun and a tin can. I tossed the can over the stern and blasted it before it hit the water. Mr. Gendarme's eyes lit up like a child's. He wanted that gun. I wanted some more carvings, and if he could get me some, the gun was his. Maryrose relayed the message, then burst out laughing at his reply. He told her Ua Pu islanders did not carve, but he did have something very valuable to trade—a cow. Where the hell would I put a cow? Maryrose repeated the question in French. The gendarme pointed to the foredeck, and for a fleeting moment I pictured myself trying to milk old Bossy in a bounding sea. She would have to eat fish, of course, since there wouldn't be room for a couple tons of hay. I asked Maryrose to find out if he had anything else to trade. He did—his 16-year-old daughter. That tore it. I told him I was keeping my shotgun, and went back to my scrub brushes. The gendarme didn't go away empty-handed, though. He gave John two ukuleles for a gallon of Galapagos rum.

While working on the boat, I had tied the Avon to the stern pulpit—loosely, evidently, for I looked up to see the dinghy adrift. It was floating across the harbor toward a coral reef, the only thing between it and the open sea. If the reef didn't catch it, we would be in the middle of the Pacific without a dinghy, far more serious than being up a creek without a paddle.

I dived off the stern of *Molly Brown* and swam after the runaway rubber boat. After a few minutes of freestyling, I realized I had miscalculated the distance to the reef and the rate the Avon was traveling. But tired as I was, I couldn't turn back, for both wind and sea were against me. At this point I couldn't have cared less about the dinghy; all I wanted was to climb up on those rocks. I don't think I could have reached them if it hadn't been for my kids at home.

The dinghy was lodged against the rocks. Trembling and vomiting, I fell into it and lay there for an hour.

We went ashore in the afternoon to watch a soccer game between a team of barefoot islanders and the crew from the trader. The sailors didn't wear shoes either. The playing field was volcanic ash, a texture somewhere between coarse sandpaper and ground glass. Everybody on the island turned out to see the contest, which was as about as brutal as anything I had seen this side of a bullring. That pleased the spectators mightily, including the island chief, who was yelling and drinking all through the match. In other words, he got roaring drunk.

It was our misfortune to meet the chief on the way back to *Molly Brown*. After a few courtesies, more or less, he proceeded to give Maryrose hell for not attending church on the island that morning. She spit and sputtered a few seconds, like a fuse on a dynamite charge, then exploded all over him with plain and fancy profanities in French, English, and assorted dialects. She concluded her remarks by telling the chief that instead of going to church in the morning and getting drunk in the afternoon, he should be setting a good example for his people. His people, most of whom had crowded around to witness the debate, encouraged her to pour it on. I think if Maryrose had decided to stay, they would have crowned her queen of Ua Pu. And so, with the sun sinking in the west and the islanders bidding us fond adieus, we took our leave of the beautiful Marquesas. To be more specific, we motored out of the harbor at about six o'clock and set a course for Tahiti, 800 miles to the southwest. Across our route stretched the Tuamotu Archipelago, a vast chain of coral atolls whose Polynesian name means "cloud of islands." Its treacherous, unmarked passages suggest a less romantic name—graveyard of the Pacific.

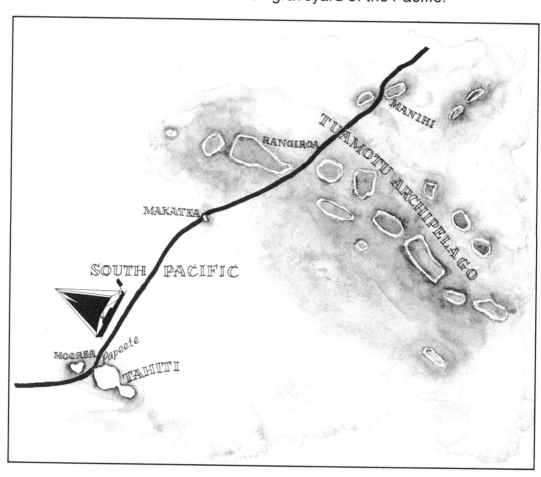

Chapter 4

Monday,
September 15:
We have ham and eggs and grits for breakfast,
and I think I'm back in southern Maryland. We are
becalmed all morning. I choose to wait for a breeze
rather than use our gas; we might have greater need
for it later. At 1500, still no breeze. At 1800 the sea is
as flat as glass; I could shave by it. At 2100 we haven't
moved.

Tuesday,
September 16:
By popular demand, we repeat yesterday's
breakfast. One of the eggs, however, has a chicken in
it. I thought we had used all those Galapagos eggs.
The sea is still very calm. And so am I. I study charts,
review my portfolio, bite my fingernails. At 1400 a light
breeze springs up out of the north. I get a celestial fix
at 1800 that shows we've made little more than a
hundred miles since Sunday evening. I can row faster
than that.

Wednesday,
September 17:
Becalmed again. Somebody get out and push.

Thursday,
September 18:
Yesterday's run was 30 miles, our worst yet.
The way things look, we may break that record today. I
spend the day reading *Kon-Tiki*, and find myself
disagreeing with Heyerdahl's supposition that the

Polynesians originally came from South America. To my unscientific eye, they look like they were cast in a separate mold. Even if there is a family connection between native islanders and mainland Indians, I think that the parent stock could just have easily originated in some Garden of Eden on a tropical isle. Thinking on such things tires me, and I seek diversion where the action is. Tunas are jumping like porpoises in our wake, and I decide to drag a lure. Move over, John. The quest is fruitless—or fishless—a real drag. By damn, I will shoot a fish if I can't catch one, and I get my shotgun and blast away. I miss, I do not even scare the fish. They keep following as if to taunt me. Night falls, and we hang a lantern on the stern—a beacon to guide out pursuers to their fate. No takers. I quit for the night, but John, undaunted and ever vigilant, stays at his post, for this is war, and he will not retreat.

Friday, September 19: We breakfast on a fine jack tuna John caught last night. A morning breeze fills our sails. At 1500 we bang into a squall and quickly out of it, entering another calm—the lull after the storm. Maryrose, defying all odds, catches a second snake mackerel. I photograph it before committing it to the hot cooking oil. A star fix locates our position 90 miles northeast of Manihi in the Tuamotus. In bright moonlight we sit on the cabin top and talk about the good times. On such a still night, sounds are magnified and imaginations intensified. Do we hear a noise out there or not? We listen, and it comes again—a steady whooshing sound, something like wind blowing through the trees. But there is hardly enough air to fill our mainsail, and we can't see the trees for the water. The sound dies, starts again in half a minute, draws closer and still closer. What the hell is out there? John spots it first, a huge, black silhouette astern, rolling in our wake, looking us over, blowing and going—a mere whale of undetermined tonnage.

Saturday,
September 20:

In a light easterly we average 2½ knots in seven hours. We are within 40 miles of Manihi, if I read the stars right. All hands agree we should stop and stretch our legs.

Sunday,
September 21:

A star fix at 0530 places us about ten miles out. I scan with the glasses but see nothing but water and sky. You have to be right on top of these flat atolls before you can see them. Landfall is an hour later, at least I hope it's land. What I see resembles fish traps in Chesapeake Bay. We draw closer and palm trees come into focus. They appear to be growing straight out of the water. I have no charts of Manihi, but the entrance is well-described in South Pacific Sailing Directions. To range in on the channel, I must pick out the red roof of a church and a flagpole and split the difference. Done, and done. We drop sail, start the engine, and make for the narrow channel. I ask John to go up on the foredeck and watch for coral, easily seen in the clear, blue water. He says, "No dice." If I want to sink *Molly Brown,* it's my business, and he wants no part of it. You are, he says, a fool to be going in there without a pilot, I may be a fool, I tell him, but I'm not stupid. No pilot—if, indeed, there is one in the islands—would waste his time on a 35-foot sailboat. And I don't choose to wait a week to prove the point. Maryrose volunteers to be the lookout, and we thread our way through the reef without a scratch. We enter a lagoon that would make a poet out of a pirate, a saint out of a sinner. Under its spell, John and I forget our animosity. We swing around to the quay in front of the village, on the western rim of the atoll.

We tied up at 2 P.M., and within minutes kids were scrambling all over the boat. They were waiting for the schooner, which pulled up shortly, that would take them to the neighboring island of Rangiroa for the school term. Mothers and fathers and friends, many with wet eyes, clustered on the quay to see the little ones off. They would be away for several months. In the melee we met Bruce and Bev Gillison, a young Australian couple who managed a pearl farm on the island. They asked us if we would like to see the pet sharks and, of course, we said yes. We walked to a small pond dug out of the coral and saw a half-dozen creatures, each about five or six feet in length, lying motionless in the water, their noses pressed against the coral wall. Bruce called them "sleepy sharks." They didn't doze long. A small boy jumped into the pool and grabbed one by the tail. They began thrashing around to beat hell, and the lad scrambled out, which I thought was wise. The sharks took a victory lap around the pool, then nosed back to the wall.

I should have known what to expect next, but if I had I couldn't have stopped Maryrose. She jumped in, twisted a shark's tail, and, upstaging the kid, remained in the water a few seconds to watch the action. That endeared her to the Polynesian onlookers and won her a dirty look from John. But he had been cool toward her ever since she caught the second snake mackerel.

Except for the sharks, there was not a lot to see on the atoll. It had little vegetation, certainly nothing to compare with the luxurient gardens we saw in the Marquesas. All the food was shipped in. As Bruce wisecracked, "Tomatoes don't grow in the Tuamotus." He invited us to his home that evening for dinner, and we came bearing a precious gift—my last bottle of Courvoisier. Bearded Jacques Moulin, owner of the pearl farm, was there, as was Coco, a roly-poly Polynesian who told Polynesian stories that must have lost something in the translating.

By 11 P.M. the brandy was gone, and I thought we should be on our way, despite the Gillisons' pleas that we stay over another day and visit the pearl farm.

As we walked to the quay, John remarked that I'd had too much to drink and was in no condition to steer us through the coral reef. When we reached the boat, he dug in his heels and announced that he wasn't going. Maryrose hopped aboard; I cast off the lines, stepped aboard myself, and shoved *Molly Brown* off. Suddenly John must have realized where he was, for, in the next instant, he was sailing through the air like a flying fish. It was truly an olympian leap. He picked himself off the deck and went below without a word. I started the motor and, drunk or not, jockeyed *Molly Brown* cleanly through the pass.

Monday, September 22: Maryrose wakes me at 0900 for breakfast. We are in a dead calm, which she likes because it's the only time she doesn't get seasick. Sitting on a glassy sea with sails flopping makes me ill. I drop the main and go to power. We motor all day, rounding the eastern tip of Rangiroa at 1800. It's 200 miles to Tahiti, and we will never make it without a breeze. Not enough fuel. I search the Sailing Directions for a gas station. The best ship-repair facilities in the French South Pacific, it says here, are at Makatea, an island 70 miles southwest, the direction we're heading. A phosphate company on the island employs 2300 people. Sounds like a good place to fill 'er up. If we get there. The engine cuts out at 1830, and I tear into the carburetor. Underway again at 2000. I stand the first watch.

Tuesday, September 23: Landfall at 1030. The island sticks way up out of the water, like a mesa in a desert. We approach from the northeast, skirting a rock cliff that forms a profile of a human face. It looks like Lyndon Johnson. Swinging around to the western side, we see a long conveyor on scaffolding, a sloping covered-bridge structure that juts from the island over a fringe of coral to deep water. Large buildings overlook the inlet. A radio mast rises atop a cliff. Huge moorings float in the lee of the island. We nose *Molly Brown* up to a mooring at the foot of the conveyor and secure her, giving her plenty of line so she will ride well away. John pumps up the Avon, and we prepare to go ashore.

Despite the appearance of heavy industry on the island, I sensed something was wrong. While rowing in, it came to me: There were no signs of life—no ships, no people, not a damned sound except the sea breaking on the reef. The island seemed as deserted as a Colorado ghost town.

But it wasn't. As we probed along the coral seeking an opening into the inlet, a voice rang out from the conveyor. "Me chief! Me chief!" We looked up to see a man waving. He pointed to a passage where we could squeeze the dinghy through. By the time we had crossed the inlet and reached a concrete bulkhead, our hailer was down to greet us. A lean Polynesian in his mid-forties, he introduced himself as Chief Virtura. The chief wore western work clothes and a wide grin.

Maryrose asked him if we could get gasoline on the island. He said we could have all we wanted, but we would have to ride the train to get it. A train? On this pimple in the Pacific? I asked Maryrose if she had heard right. French words flew back and forth. Translation: There is a train, and at the end of the line is gas. Would we care to take a ride? Well, I guess we would. I hadn't been on a train since a high school outing to Harpers Ferry on the B&O.

We climbed a long, steep flight of stairs to the top of the cliff. There was no talking during the heart-pounding ascent. Everybody, with the exception of the chief, who was used to such calisthenics, was too busy inhaling and exhaling and, in my case, fighting off vertigo. By the time I reached the last step, my legs felt like they were encased in concrete boots, my head like it was stuffed with feathers. After a suitable pause to slow pulse rates, we walked along the brink of the cliff, from where I had literally a bird's-eye view of *Molly Brown,* 2000 feet below. She looked no bigger than a peanut. It was hard to comprehend that the little boat had carried me 7,000 miles, harder still to believe it had brought me here—a tiny island two miles wide and five miles long with its own railroad.

Up until two years ago, the chief told us, Makatea was a booming place, with hundreds of European and Chinese workers. They departed when *Compagnie Francaise des Phosphates Oceanic,* a French mining outfit, did not renew its 50-year lease, having removed most of the island's rich lode of phosphate. Left behind were yawning pits, antiquated equipment, and a number of well-built homes. Chief Virtura and his band of 160 Polynesians moved out of their thatched huts into these houses; in fact, there was a housing surplus, and some families maintained homes at each end of the island.

The chief's main home, spacious, tidy, and surrounded by flowers, had once served as offices for the mining company. Alongside it ran a narrow-gauge railroad track; and, sure enough, there sat the train—a small diesel locomotive and a tin-roofed flatcar equipped with six or eight benches. The chief bade us take seats, called out his family, and started the engine. One of his many sons, a lad of about ten, climbed into the cab beside him and dropped the little locomotive in gear. The Makatea Express was on its way.

The chief was a super guy. He would stop the train every few minutes to let somebody off or give a lift to a copra worker or a fisherman returning home. Nor would he pass up children scurrying out of their homes and eager for a train ride. The sun was low in the west when we reached Chief Virtura's number two house, where he kept his motorcycle. How he acquired that item I have no idea, but I was glad he had. It was the only gasoline-powered vehicle on the island. From its fuel supply, a full 50-gallon drum, we siphoned off 20 gallons of gas into four jerry jugs we'd had the foresight to bring along. Then we chugged back across the island, where the chief had some of his men carry the cans down the long stairway. We wedged two of them in the Avon, the chief and his brother-in-law Jean carrying the other pair in an outrigger canoe. Twenty minutes later they were safely stowed on *Molly Brown.* A friendly farewell, a few bucks for the chief, and we would be on our way. Or so I thought.

But our Polynesian guests, as fascinated with our boat as we had been with their train, were in no hurry to leave. To slake their thirst—and ours—I uncorked a jug of Galapagos rum, which was still in good supply, and a bottle of wine. The evening wore on. The rum began to work. Jean, under the influence, favored us with song after song, accompanying himself on one of John's ukuleles. He had, he owned, performed for an audience before, having toured Europe with a Polynesian dance group.

After he finished, I got up to say thank you and goodbye. But first a few words from the chief. He set down his glass and told us that *Molly Brown* was the first yacht to call at Makatea in almost two years. He had fond memories of the last boat, for it took a sick child from the island to a hospital in Tahiti. The youngster, though near death, recovered and was brought home several weeks later on the same yacht. The chief got a little dewy-eyed then and went on to tell us how the crew of the mercy boat received the red-carpet treatment, Polynesian style. It must have been something. They stayed in Makatea for six months.

While we had done absolutely nothing to deserve it, the chief decided on the spot to honor us in similar fashion. He declared tomorrow a holiday. Jean was told to have two pigs killed in the morning and prepare a feast. While the meat cooked, the chief would take us on a grand tour of the island. I looked at my watch and sat down. Though anxious to be underway now that we had gas, I couldn't decline such a generous invitation. Besides, it might be a long time before I rode another train. As our friends swung over the side into their canoe, I promised them we would see them at eight o'clock in the morning. After they left, I unbolted *Molly Brown*'s brass fog bell and stuffed it in a paper sack.

Maryrose was up at seven with breakfast going. I rolled out and shook John awake, which he didn't appreciate. He said he preferred to sleep. I reminded him that the chief would be expecting us at eight, and we weren't going to stand him up—so, get your ass out of bed. He grumbled, but he got up.

The chief met us at the foot of the stairs, and once again we scaled the heights. When we reached the little engine, I dipped into the paper bag I had brought, pulled out the brass bell, and mounted it on the cab, outside the window, within easy reach of the engineer. We climbed aboard, and as the train started rolling, the chief, beaming like a sweepstakes winner, stuck out his arm and yanked on the bell. He seldom stopped ringing it for the rest of the ride.

The morning rushed by as we toured the abandoned mine and processing plant, the coconut drying sheds (copra is the island's only export), and the schoolhouse at the far end of the island, where two Polynesian women taught about 20 children. Attentive and neatly dressed, they all stood as we entered the room. Before we left, Chief Virtura told the teachers to dismiss the kids for the rest of the day, and invited them to attend the feast.

It was mid-afternoon when we returned to his house, ding-donging all the way. The entire population of the island had showed up, and I must have shook hands with all 160. I felt like a politician hustling votes. The only thing wanting was a brass band, although swinging Jean did his best to make up for the lack. Well-oiled from swigging tuba, a fermented coconut brew with the kick of a draft horse, he sang and danced until thirst overtook him again.

The feast was informal and filling. Wrapped in palm leaves, placed in a pit, and covered with a blanket of hot coals, the pigs cooked all day, simmering in their juices and splitting their skins. If you fancy succulent pork—and I sure do—you won't find any better than Makatea roast pig.

Many of the islanders, the chief in the lead, walked with us downstairs to the bulkhead—and that was about the only good thing about leaving: I wouldn't have to climb those damned steps again. On the other hand, I didn't see how we could get to *Molly Brown.* The wind had come in fresh, kicking up seas that crashed over the reef and into the inlet. One look told me it would be suicide to try paddling a rubber boat through that wild surf. While I stared at *Molly Brown* bouncing drunkenly on the waves and worried that her mooring lines would chafe through, Chief Virtura disappeared. Shortly he returned with an old man who, the chief said, would take us out to *Molly Brown.* How I didn't know, but I wasn't about to question these resourceful people. The old man shuffled off to an equipment shed and came out shouldering a 70-horsepower Mercury outboard engine, a load that would have taxed the strength of a man half his age. What a stud he must have been in his prime. He needed help for the next item procured from the shed—a heavy 16-foot fishing boat. It took four of us to wheel it on a cart to the bulkhead and slide it into the water.

Tying the Avon behind, we got into the boat, and the old man started the engine. He waited a minute for the sea to please him, then leaned on the throttle. As we shot into the foaming inlet, a breaker reached up and slapped me in the face. I needed that. Despite its resemblance to a rapidly filling bathtub, the wooden boat plowed through the inlet, past the reef, into relatively calmer water, where the old man throttled her back and set her smartly alongside *Molly Brown*.

At 6 P.M. we were under sail for Tahiti, 130 miles away. With a stiff breeze out of the northeast, I thought we might not need the gas that compelled us to stop here in the first place. But need it or not, I was glad we hadn't bypassed Makatea.

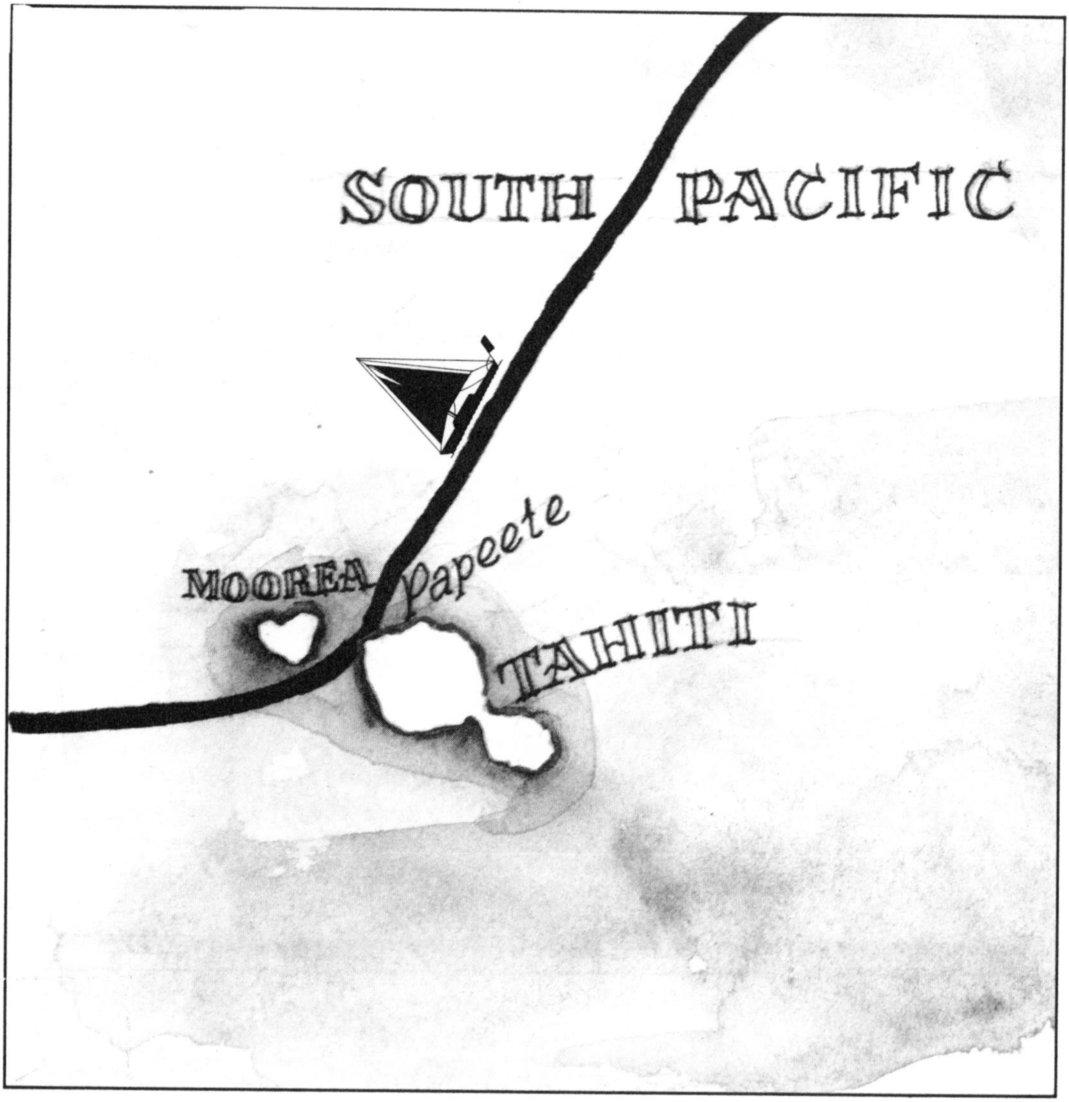
SOUTH PACIFIC
MOOREA
Papeete
TAHITI

Chapter 5

Thursday,
September 25:

The sea is as flat as a pool table, and we are motoring. Have been all night. But we do have canvas up—an awning, to protect us from the searing sun and, at 1400, a rain squall. At dusk we pick up the lights of Tahiti.

Friday,
September 26:

At 0300 we round Point Venus, coast along the reef to red and green flashing lights marking Passe de Papeete, and drop anchor in the harbor. Exhilarated at making port but too tired to wait for the dawn, I fall into my bunk. Two hours later a blast from the pilot boat's horn splits the air, and the French harbormaster bounds aboard breathing fire. That naturally ignites Maryrose, already indignant at having her sleep interrupted. After she tells him off, he tells us we have anchored in the channel, which is not the best place to be. I take the hint and move *Molly Brown* to a quay, remembering to do it backward like the man said. That is, anchoring with the bow out and the stern in, bridging the gap by gangplank. After breakfast, Gigi, the friendly Tahitian policeman, comes aboard with the usual forms for us to fill out. At 0900 we step ashore.

Tahiti has a mountain a mile and a half high,

black sand beaches, orchids growing as thick as dandelions in a Maryland meadow, and good-looking women. It also has too many automobiles, thousands of bicycles, a jet airport, and swank hotels and restaurants. But most important, it has ice! I had not seen a bag of ice since we left Panama. So what's the first thing I did in Papeete? I went to a grass-roofed sidewalk café and ordered a cup of hot coffee.

While I sipped it, I found myself thinking instead of relaxing. Ahead lay the rest of the South Pacific, the Indian Ocean, the wide Atlantic—a hell of a lot of territory to cover within a year. The biggest problem was weather. Although I counted on reaching Australia before the height of the hurricane season, I would be sailing the Indian Ocean at monsoon time. When, and if, I completed that passage in one piece, I would have to turn the corner at Good Hope in winter, which is the gale season. My timing was bad, but there was no sense in worrying. Come high winds and high water, I was still determined to go for all 360 degrees. Right now, however, I was in Tahiti, and Tahiti is no place to worry about anything.

I planned to spend a week here and ended up staying almost two. Some visitors are reluctant to leave Tahiti at all; but, as Maryrose and John discovered, the French authorities don't encourage homesteading. Maryrose wondered if she might find a job in Papeete. Gigi told her to forget it—too many workers, not enough work. That depressed her spirits a bit, so she and I took a walk along the beach and tried to figure something out.

Maryrose told me she had run away from home when she was 17, and she had been aimlessly knocking around the world ever since. She had worked at dozens of menial jobs, none of them for very long, none of them very rewarding. But she was a good worker; I could vouch for that. Even though seasick almost constantly, she kept *Molly Brown* as clean as a whistle, whether in port or at sea; and she was handy in the galley, coming up with tasty meals despite the drawbacks of a small boat. True, she could be abrasive—a real hellcat at times—especially around pompous port officials for whom she had no respect. I could readily understand how she felt about such people, though I was raised to always act polite, even if on the verge of hitting someone in the mouth. Maryrose was tough, smart, gutsy, a gal with a lot of character and considerable charm. I might have felt a little awkward with her at a lawn party in southern Maryland, but I couldn't have asked for a better companion on *Molly Brown*. If you would like to continue sailing with me, I told her, I would be glad to have you. She said yes, she would, and we walked to a Tahitian restaurant, the Piatate, and got something to eat.

As for John, he'd had enough of *Molly Brown* and her captain, so it came as no surprise that he wanted to spend an extra couple of weeks in Tahiti, then ship out to Australia. A dude with the ladies, he had met a cute Tahitian girl who owned a motor scooter, and the two of them would ride all day around the island, showing up at the boat for evening cocktails. That was something of a trying time for John, inasmuch as he couldn't speak French or Tahitian, and his little Tahitian girl couldn't understand a word of English. As a result, she and Maryrose passed the evening talking to each other. I did not try to change John's mind about staying; in fact, I went with him to plead his case at the immigration office. The officials agreed to grant him an extended visa on condition that he buy a steamship ticket, which he did. Then he rented a room on the third floor of a small hotel overlooking the harbor. I think the arrangement worked out well for all concerned.

There were 15 or 20 boats in the harbor, and we met some of the crews. The oddest boat of the bunch was a New Zealand-built ferro-cement job, which interested me greatly, since I had a cement background. It never dawned on me while in the contracting business to build boats out of the stuff; if it had, I might have tried it and gone bust that way. In any event, crew members John Benjamin from Auckland, New Zealand, and Peter Novak from Sydney said ferro-cement boats were popular down under. The skipper, an ascetic Frenchman, was as odd as his boat. A vegetarian with a liking for fresh seaweed, he told us one night—with Maryrose interpreting—about the little men he had met from outer space. They landed beside him at sea and took him for rides in their spaceship, which, I presumed, was not constructed of cement. I sat in the cockpit trying to look half-way intelligent while he ranted on, apparently dead serious, and Maryrose, seemingly awestruck, translated. I could not tell if he was putting her on, if she was putting me on, or if they were both nuts. Peter and John said they were getting off the cement boat in Tahiti if they had to swim out.

John Tucker invited two Pan American airline pilots aboard for drinks one night, and they, I suspect, concluded that *we* were crazy. Laying over a couple of days before returning to the West Coast, they marveled at, but did not envy, our island hopping in a small boat. Much simpler to fly now and pay later. They had a point. But, hell, I had one too. And that was, if you fail at something, like your life, up the ante and shoot it all. I wasn't going just somewhere, I was going for broke. And, unlike the poor yachty, I was going first class all the way. That is, as long as the grits held out.

Speaking of food, Maryrose, John, and I treated

ourselves to lamb chops at Club Tahiti the following evening. At the table next to us sat an elderly American couple. They told us they were traveling around the world via Pan Am. We told them we were doing the same thing on a sailboat. They wanted to know all about our voyage across the Pacific, and we obliged by telling them everything—from catching the second and third snake mackerels ever taken on a line to riding a train on Makatea. They didn't believe our story; we were joshing them. No, we insisted, it's all true, the part about the donkeys eating oranges, even the part about the pet sharks. They smiled and shook their heads: We hadn't sailed a boat across the Pacific. I finally admitted we made the whole thing up, and the truth was that we'd had the boat flown out and were cruising around Tahiti. That's more like it, they said.

I invited them to come down to *Molly Brown* next afternoon for a drink. They came, they saw the salty little boat, and they were convinced at last that we had sailed her across the Pacific. By chance, we would later meet them in Australia. After leaving Tahiti, they told us, they always checked the docks in port cities they visited. And they would look for *Molly Brown*.

Our last several days on Tahiti were more work than play. While Maryrose shopped for groceries, I tore into *Molly Brown*'s vital parts, dismantling the bow pulpit, where salt water had seeped through and corroded wires of the running lights. Another task was to find replacements for two winch handles lost overboard. I spent half a day looking and came up empty-handed. So, robbing Peter to pay Paul, I took one of the large handles from the cockpit winch and had it machined down to fit the winch for the main halyard. Finding a new self-steerer blade was out of the question, but I thought I might get one made by using the old patched blade as a model. A craftsman at the boatyard said he could do the job—and he wouldn't need my broken blade to guide him. "How?" I wondered aloud, for these things have to be right on the money. He disappeared into the back of his shop and returned with a worm-eaten old blade identical to mine. "Where the hell did you get that?" I asked. From an American yacht, he told me; he had made a new blade for it a couple of weeks ago. He even remembered the boat's name. *La Salle.*

At this time, I was more meticulous about having everything in good working order than I was later. I did not know that you could always get from port to port by sheer instinct for self-preservation— and, of course, a bit of luck. If charts were available and the running lights worked, okay. If not, it was still okay. You just made do and enjoyed the scenery.

Friday, October 3, the day before our departure, I borrowed a fenderless bicycle and toured Papeete, pronounced poppy-yaytay. But no matter how you say it, it's a spellbinding place. Trade winds murmured through breadfruit trees, country girls with baskets in hand and gardenias in their hair paraded like queens to the open-air market, jitney busses festooned with flowers and blazoned with names such as "Tickle-Tickle" rumbled down the avenue scattering bikers and hikers. A Polynesian man leaning against a stucco wall smiled and strummed his guitar. A Chinese storekeeper stood in his doorway and scanned for customers. The whine of a jet overhead broke the spell. I biked to the post office, to customs, to immigration, across the bridge to the port captain's office. Then, clearance papers in my pocket, I peddled back to the waterfront and lunched on oysters and beer at the Vaima café. It was a happy time, yet a sad time, for tomorrow I would be leaving this enchanted island.

One chore remained, and that afternoon I got to it. The dinghy, sitting in the water next to *Molly Brown*, had picked up a coating of oil. I brought it up onto the quay, where there was a hose, and began scrubbing off the gunk. Pretty soon, a short, balding American in a Hawaiian sports shirt walked up and asked if I was captain of *Molly Brown*. I said I was. Why? He explained that he owned a small island about 30 miles out, and he would like to charter my boat to visit it. I told him *Molly Brown* wasn't for charter. He implored me to change my mind. I couldn't, I said, because I was already cleared to leave Papeete in the morning, and I didn't want to go through that red tape again. I suggested he try one of the other sailboats in the harbor. Better, charter a power boat; that could run you out to your island real quick. He said no, he had to have a sailboat, and it had to be *Molly Brown*. He was damned insistent about it. I told him again, flatly and with finality, that *Molly Brown* wasn't for hire. He wanted to know where I was going in such a big hurry. I told him the Cooks. He said I was crazy to be going to the Cooks now; it was the middle of the hurricane season there. I said that one of us was mistaken, and I didn't think it was me, because I had been studying the pilot charts, and they didn't show any storm lines in the area. That failed to impress him. He claimed that he had been in the Cooks about this time a couple of years ago, and got hit with a terrible hurricane. I said that was odd, because the storm wasn't diagrammed on the pilot charts. After that, we got into an argument.

It ended with him stalking off mumbling that he hoped I made it, though he seemed fairly certain I wouldn't. I said I hope so too, fella, and went back to my scrubbing. After he left, a girl on the next boat yelled: "What were you and Marlon Brando arguing about?" I thought that guy looked familiar.

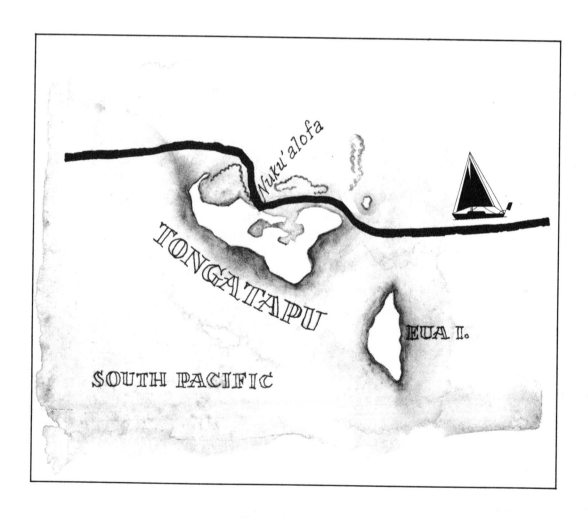

Chapter 6

Saturday, October 4:	We grab a few bags of ice and depart Papeete at 1330. John came down to see us off and wish us luck. Our destination is Rarotonga in the Cook Islands, about 600 miles to the southwest. We should make it in five days. The wind is west-northwest at force three, and *Molly Brown* is moving well under the main and No. 1 genny. At 2300 I check the self-steerer and go to bed.
Sunday, October 5:	I arise at 0630 to find us aback and becalmed. The wind is fluky and we're on the wrong tack. I tack, find air, but not much. At 1130 the wind freshens out of the southeast, building to a steady force four. By evening it is too cloudy for a fix and too rough to make dinner. I have a cold beer and go to bed hungry. Maryrose is not hungry; she is seasick.
Monday, October 6:	It's still cloudy and windy, but the barometer is rising. We have passed through a slight depression. At 1000 we see the sun. After lunch, Maryrose takes up John's old post and baits a line. To conserve tackle, we don't use a fishing rod but an inner tube, tying the line to the tube to absorb the shock when we get a strike. Even so, we still lose a lot of tackle. No sooner

said than done. Maryrose hooks a big one. We can't pull it in hand over hand, so we wrap the line around the genoa winch in the cockpit and start cranking the monster in. My God, it's a shark. We pull him right up to the boat, then he snaps the line like it was a piece of spaghetti. John, you pisciphobe, you should have been here. I shoot the stars at 1900, which tells me we're almost halfway to Rarotonga.

Tuesday, October 7:

I'm up at 0400 to see if everything is in good shape. The main is up, we are on port tack, and the wind is backing to the southeast. That could spell trouble if it keeps up. I go back to bed and sleep until 0800. Now the wind has backed all the way around to the east and freshened some. As a result, the self-steerer has us veering to the northwest, and I don't want any northing. I drop the main and go on No. 2 genny alone. At 1500 we are becalmed for half an hour. Back up goes the main. But not for long. Here comes the wind, and hard. Down comes the main; up goes the storm jib. I damn near get blown off the deck. This is a real howler. Maybe Brando was right. By dusk the wind is blowing at 40 knots, and the seas are so high I'm afraid they will break over the stern and drown us. I put the hatch boards in, then sit in the cockpit with the safety harness on and wait for the worst. It comes, a whole mountain range of liquid Mount Everests. But *Molly Brown* is a mountain climber. Every time a big wall of water rolls up to her transom, she picks right up and lets it roll under her. Convinced she will ride out the gale, I go down at midnight to get some sleep.

Wednesday, October 8:

At 0700 the wind has moderated to force five, but the seas are still high, and it's raining. I pick up an assortment of books, clothes, and canned goods that have been reshuffled by the buffeting. A little water has seeped in through ports and hatches—nothing to worry about. I make coffee, which is not easy in a bouncing boat. I drink it fast, before it sloshes out of the cup. The wind blows all day, and the seas keep knocking us about. It's an odd feeling to stagger around like this and be cold sober. I don't touch the sextant, but I do get an RDF line at 2100 from Aitutaki Atoll, a good 150 miles north of Rarotonga. One line doesn't give position, but it does show which way the island is bearing. Right now, I guess we are well north of Rarotonga, the only decent port in the Cooks. I change course to due west.

Thursday, October 9: It's a clear morning, and the seas aren't quite so bad. At 0830 I dead reckon we are 500 miles out of Tahiti and almost on the same longitude as Rarotonga. But the storm has kicked us way north. With the wind out of the south at force five, we would have to beat into it all the way down to Rarotonga. To hell with the Cooks. We'll run right on to Tonga, even if it is another thousand miles. I would rather reach a thousand than beat a hundred.

Friday, October 10: This is more like it—clear sky, moderate sea, steady force four breeze out of the southeast. A morning RDF line puts Aitutaki behind us. Good sailing all day. Clouds blot out the stars, so no fix. Maryrose, worn out, goes straight to bed after dinner. She talks in her sleep—in French.

Saturday, October 11: I'm up at 0700 and find trouble. During the night the wind backed to the northeast, causing the mainsail to jibe and the boom vang to break. (The boom vang is the strap that holds the boom down.) And the taffrail log is minus its spinner. A hungry shark must have bitten it off. At noon I get a fix, which puts us 750 miles out and 750 to go. Our breeze dies, and I try to start the engine for the first time in more than a week. Predictably, it won't start. I take the carburetor out, clean it, take the plugs out, dry them; then I put everything back together and say magic cuss words. It starts. It always starts if I fool with it long enough.

Sunday, October 12:
I'm up half the night tinkering with the engine. It runs awhile, then cuts out. I get it running again at about 0300, and a squall hits. A fresh southerly an hour later permits me to put up the main and go to bed. I sleep until 1030. Maryrose complains that I snore. In the afternoon the sky becomes overcast, and the wind honks up to force four. I drop the main and set the working jib, which we will run with through the night.

Monday, October 13:
It's a beautiful, clearing morning. At 0530 I shoot the stars and hoist the mainsail. At noon I get a sun line. At 1730 I get another celestial fix. My chart is covered with a maze of directional lines plotted over the last ten days. I'm a lousy navigator. *Molly Brown* has been zigzagging all over the ocean.

Wednesday, October 15:
Yesterday was good sailing. Today is better. Hash and eggs for breakfast, but no grits. They're all gone. We have been out 11 days and made about a thousand miles—nothing to brag about, but we're getting there.

Thursday, October 16:
Warm, sunny, breezy—the prettiest day we've had since leaving Papeete. A fix at 1900 puts us 100 miles out of Tongatapu, the main island in the Tongas. My chart shows them scattered over an area larger than the state of Maryland. I do not have a chart of Nuku'alofa, the harbor of Tongatapu, but I'll try to read my way in with the South Pacific Sailing Directions.

Friday, October 17:
I wake up at 0500 and look into the morning haze. No land in sight. I go back to bed. Up again at 0730, and there's still nothing on the horizon. I switch on the radio. Polynesian music! They're playing our song. As usual when nearing a port, Maryrose is tidying up. She wants *Molly Brown* to be spotless. At 1015 I make a landfall, but what I see are high peaks, which makes me wonder where the hell we are.

Tongatapu is supposed to be a flat island covered with pine trees. Back to the Sailing Directions. Half an hour later I figure it out: We're off Eua Island, 30 miles south of Tongatapu. That's maddening, since I had concentrated on being high. We work up along Eua, sight Tongatapu, and keep sailing northerly. There's a passage through the reef somewhere here, but it's getting late, and I don't want to chance it in the dark. I work in behind the northeasternmost edge of the reef and drop anchor. This has been a tiring trip. I've lost at least 20 pounds, most of it in the past two weeks. It will be good to go ashore again and fatten up. This ought to be the place to do it. Tonga is ruled by a king who weighs 350 pounds.

Sunday, October 19: Up at 0500 and, after an hour's worth of carburetor adjusting, we motor toward Nuku'alofa, losing Saturday in the process. We cross the International Date Line and enter the reef-enclosed harbor, coasting past the royal palace. A red-roofed, white frame building with a cupola and lots of gingerbread trim, it resembles one of those old Ocean City hotels on the boardwalk. A power launch painted brilliant green—it looks like a Grand Banks trawler—comes out to meet us. We are directed to a quay where a British frigate, her guns glistening in the afternoon sun, is waiting for the king to come aboard and review the crew. We must wait for the immigration officer and health inspector. Friendly fellows in white shirts, brown skirts, and aprons woven of pandanus leaves—traditional dress—they find everything in order and give us the go-ahead. I move *Molly Brown* to a cozy little basin and tie her next to several fishing boats. That warship dwarfed her. As luck would have it, there is a shower nearby and also a bar. I have a cold beer, a shower, and another beer, the last with Maryrose, who joins me after her bath. A little soap and fresh water is a welcome treat after two weeks at sea. For one thing, it makes you smell better. We start to walk toward the center of town when a jeeplike taxi pulls up looking for a fare. We jump into the back of the mini-moke, as these springless vehicles are called, and off we go past white wooden houses behind white picket fences. The largest, newest building in Nuku'alofa is the Dateline Hotel on the waterfront, and that's where we spend the rest of the evening, dining on steak and potatoes and a bottle of red wine. We're drinking brandy at the bar when a helicopter pilot named Peter comes over. He's from the Australian research ship *Craystar,* a rusty, 300-footer we had seen coming in. The first mate and the mechanic soon join the party, doubtless attracted by Maryrose, the only female around who isn't waiting tables. We swap yarns, learn more about Australia than we care to know, then mini-moke back to *Molly Brown* at midnight.

Monday, October 20:

I wake up thinking I'm back down on my father's farm in Upper Marlboro. Roosters are crowing. Where there are roosters, there must be hens and likewise eggs, which I have not tasted for some days. Maryrose and I remedy that at the little restaurant-bar near the quay, then stroll into town, poking into shops along the way, chatting with the people. I have no language problem here, for Tonga, a British protectorate, has known English words and ways since Captain James Cook explored the islands two centuries ago. Dodging bikes and motor scooters, we hike up to the palace. I start to go in and sign the guest book when one of the royal guards politely turns me away. But hang around, he says, and I'll tell you all about Tonga right after the changing of the guard. That modest ceremony takes place presently, and big Bill Musso in dress whites—shirt and skirt— comes over and sits beside us on the grass. He's an expert on Tonga, having never been anywhere else in his life.

We invite him to the boat that evening, which pleases him immensely. He promises to bring some chicken cooked Polynesian style. Later we meet Peter and the mechanic at the Dateline bar, and they agree to come too. Bill Musso shows up with two attractive Tongan girls and the chicken. I supply the whiskey.

Our dinner party in the cabin is going smoothly, when Maryrose hears a noise in the forward cabin. She opens the door, and there is a Polynesian tossing her clothes through the forward hatch onto the deck. One glance tells Bill all he needs to know. He's out of the cabin, up the companionway, and on deck in practically a single motion, arriving just as the thief comes up through the hatch. Bill throws one awesome punch, knocking the guy off the boat and into the water. Two Polynesian men standing on the dock fish him out. For a minute or two I think Bill must have killed him, but he finally moves. We return to the cabin to drain our glasses while Bill, who finds the incident amusing, entertains us with an instant replay.

For the next couple of days the log reads like a shopping list and a repair manual for *Molly Brown.* I'll spare you the boring details. We did some sightseeing, touring the island in a mini-moke chauffeured by a pleasant Polynesian who openly admired Americans. He had fought on our side during World War II in the battle of the Coral Sea. He was anxious to show us the blowholes on the southwest end of the island; so, after loading up with picnic supplies—a watermelon, bananas, mangos, some sweet corn, a couple loaves of bread—we bumped down the road past sparse coconut groves and thatched huts. The driver, whose name I can't pronounce, let alone spell, parked the car on the shoulder, and we carried our picnic supplies down to a patch of nice beach where some women were weaving baskets. All around us the water was spewing up through coral. This phenomenon, our guide explained, was caused by rollers tunneling into the rock and gushing through openings Old Faithful style. There were hundreds of blowholes, some of them jetting water 50 or 60 feet into the air. Our driver said there were even bigger ones farther down, but I didn't think it was worth the walk. Besides it was lunchtime. We roasted the corn in the husk—tough, like American field corn, but good—and cut the watermelon.

We continued on around the island to another Tongan attraction, a huge tree—its trunk must have been six feet thick—with drooping branches. It was a big tree all right, but I've seen big trees before, for instance the Wye oak on Maryland's Eastern Shore. No, I missed the point, my Polynesian friend protested; look what's *in* the tree. Large bats were in the tree, hundreds of them hanging upside down from every twig. From the ground they looked something like coconuts growing in the wrong places. The bats are called flying foxes and they eat fruit, but the Tongans don't seem to mind. When they run a little short, they eat the bats.

On Wednesday morning I awoke with a terrible hangover from the night before. The *Craystar* crew, endowed with a liquor supply ample enough for the Dateline Hotel, had invited us to a party the likes of which I had never before experienced. Tongan men played guitars, Tongan girls danced, and one Aussie after another set endurance records for the most booze consumed before passing out. I thought I could drink, but these guys made me look like a WCTUer. Whether any pregnancies resulted from the party, I do not know. All I can say is that the possibilities were there. Wednesday evening several members of the crew had recovered sufficiently to join Maryrose and me for dinner in an Indian restaurant. We had curried rice so hot it blistered your tongue. It took lots of cold beer to put the fire out. Thursday morning I went to the bank, cashed a few traveler's checks, bought some gas, loaded supplies, and said goodbye. At 2 P.M. we shoved off, and at seven I was in the sack dead tired. This had been an exhausting vacation.

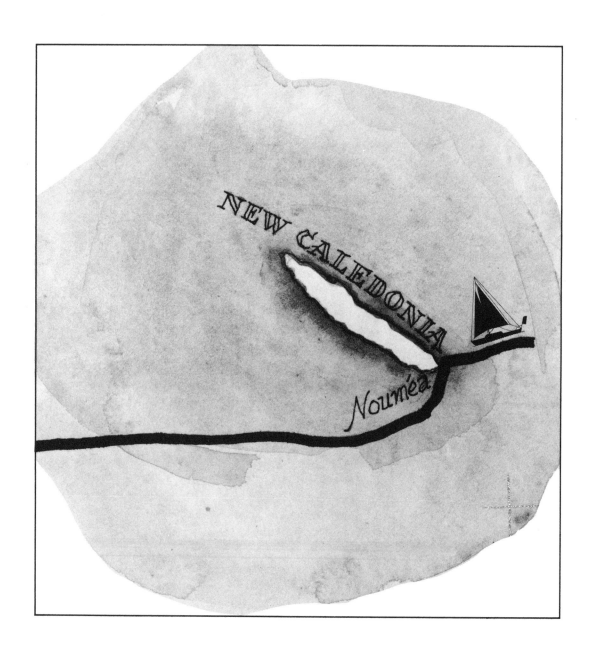

Chapter 7

Friday,
October 24:

Warm and clear, light seas, breeze out of the east. At noon I take down the main and hoist twin headsails. Maryrose, all by herself, figures out why the Tongas are called the Friendly Islands: Since the people steal from everybody, they have to be friendly; otherwise, they would all be dead.

Saturday,
October 25:

Nice day but no air. At noon I start the engine to get us around the southern Fijis. Southeast wind returns at 1400. Up goes the main and No. 2 genny. We'll stand watch through the night to look out for reefs.

Sunday,
October 26:

Main down and double headsails up. The Pacific is treating *Molly Brown* as a gentleman should treat a lady—tenderly. Early evening squall holds promise of a bath, but the rain ends before I can locate the soap. Shortwave has news. Cyclone is churning off west coast of New Caledonia.

Monday,
October 27:

I'm up at 0700 twirling the dials for a weather forecast. Nothing but static and rock-and-roll. Sometimes it's hard to tell which is which. Easy riding all day and a fix at twilight. Maryrose writes down the time from the Accutron as I shoot Rigil Kent, Vega, and Acrux. I switch on the cabin lights to work my fixes while Maryrose preheats the alcohol stove to prepare dinner. Clipboard in lap and charts and nautical almanac on the bunk beside me, I proceed to find us. After dinner it's coffee on the cabin top.

Tuesday, October 28:

We have fried tomatoes for breakfast—the last of them, Maryrose says. That's enough to ruin a man's day. I have trouble with sun lines. The evening sun line is behind the morning sun line. Surely we're not sailing backwards.

Wednesday, October 29:

I arise at 0730 and go right to work on my navigation. Good noon sight puts us 460 miles out of New Caledonia.

Thursday, October 30:

Another pretty day. I drop the main at 1400 and put up the working jib and No. 2 genny. Write letters in the evening.

Friday, October 31:

Morning sun line and noon sight right on the money. We're 200 miles out. After dinner a little action. I'm sitting on the cabin top sipping coffee as usual when a light appears on the horizon. Strange. We're not in the shipping lanes. Hello. Another light. And another. We're sailing into a whole string of them. Out of the night comes a banging sound, then a shout. I cannot get the twin poles down in time to jibe around. Grabbing a flashlight, I shine it over the side and pick out a rowboat with a lone occupant. He is frantically waving a lantern, pounding on the sides, and preparing to abandon ship. It is impossible to stop *Molly Brown,* and it would take half an hour to turn her around. We charge by, missing the rowboat by a whisker. Maryrose and I give a friendly greeting in passing and receive in return a few shrill words in Japanese. I do not understand the lantern waver, but a wild guess would be that he's referring to my ancestry. We approach a second boat, and again a lantern waves and pounding on wood is heard. Another near miss, another cheery but unappreciated salutation. We are barging through a Japanese fishing fleet with seeming wild abandon, scattering tiny boats, fouling tuna lines, and probably endangering world peace. Around midnight we clear the fleet.

"I theenk you worry about New Caledonia," Maryrose remarked next morning as I was poring over the charts. She was right. I was worried. A narrow, mountainous ridge stretching more than 200 miles in length, New Caledonia rises from the ocean like a picket fence, and guarding it on all sides is a nightmare of reefs and coral heads. Since *Molly Brown* was rapidly approaching the southeastern tip of the island, I had to figure out a way to get us into Noumea, the port on the lower west coast. Sailing Directions gave me two options. The safest was to sail 70 miles south of the island to clear the off-lying hazards, swing around to the north and sail 80 miles to an opening in the reef, then proceed across the coral patch to Noumea. In other words, detour 150 miles. The other choice was to head straight for the obstacle course at the south end of the island, picking a way through Havannah Pass and hugging the coast up to Noumea. That treacherous maze would have been a challenge for a seasoned captain who knew the waters, a foolish risk for one who didn't. "Maryrose," I said, "you want it short and sweet or long and drawn out?" She chose Havannah Pass. Why not? I thought. This will be a good warm-up for the Barrier Reef.

A star fix was a necessity that night, for I had to be damned sure of our position when we hit the coast. The fix placed *Molly Brown* 35 miles south of Ile Mare, the southernmost of the Loyalty Islands that parallel New Caledonia, and 70 miles due east of the entrance to Havannah Pass. Our position looked good. We should make the pass in the morning. Only one thing bothered me. Would the two-knot current described in the Sailing Directions take us up the coast or down? I had no way of knowing. But I should have no trouble in recognizing the entrance to the pass. The chart showed an elevation of 1980 feet.

I got up at 4:30 Sunday morning to shoot the moon. Usually I don't use the moon, but I was leary as hell of this whole damned mess. For the first time on the trip I had the feeling I was sailing *Molly Brown* into a trap. At daybreak the only thing in front of her bow was ocean. No 1980-foot cliff. We made landfall at 9 A.M.—a low island. Son of a bitch! Back to the drawing board. The best solution I could come up with was that the current had swept us 18 miles south, and this was the Isle of Pines, a small island off the southern tip of New Caledonia—like the dot of an exclamation point. If that was the case, Havannah Pass lay north. I would find out at noon, when I took a noon sight. Meantime, the only thing to do was sheet *Molly Brown* in and start working northward. At noon it was raining. Not hard; in fact, it would have been pleasant if I didn't need the sun so badly. We kept on heading north, every minute expecting the cliffs of the pass to come into view. At 1500 we sighted land off the bow, but it was another low island. And could those be reefs ahead? Yes, they could; and it would be dark in an hour. I had sailed *Molly Brown* 9,000 miles in less than five months, and I was not about to sink her tonight. "Maryrose," I said, "we are going to park. If it is clear in the morning, we will sort this mess out." I dropped the headsail, sheeted the main in, unhooked the Hasler, and lashed the helm about 15 degrees off to starboard—just enough to keep the main full without luffing, but not so much that the boat could get under way.

At 4:30 the next morning I again shot the moon. Slowly, carefully, accurately, I plotted the line on the chart. It ran east and west. I now had latitude, but it was hard to believe, for the fix showed *Molly Brown* to be ten miles north of Ile Mare and considerably farther from Havannah Pass than when we started for it. The catch was the current. It had taken us north, not south, the previous night; and, of course, like a chump I had been sailing north when we needed southing. It was all very clear now, so we set sail for Havannah Pass, 80 miles away. At midnight we saw the lights marking the pass. Deciding not to chance it in the dark, we hove to for the second night in a row.

We were underway at daybreak, dodging those 1980-foot cliffs on the right and miles of coral on the left. A fresh easterly was pushing us—a little too fresh for comfort. I wanted to drop the mainsail, as it was constantly on the verge of jibing, but I didn't think Maryrose could handle the helm of a runaway boat in a narrow channel. The western end of the pass reminded me of the Grand Canyon. We had to run the slot between a small island and the mainland, with cliffs towering on both sides. They funneled the wind behind *Molly Brown* like the blast from a rocket. If there had been a drawbridge around the bend it would have demasted her. But there wasn't, and she charged on through like the Wabash Cannonball. The wild ride came to an abrupt end when the pass opened into the coral shelf. In the lee of the island the breeze dropped as if the switch had been pulled, and we reached leisurely northward through the coral patch. While Maryrose piloted the boat, now under power, into the U-shaped harbor of Noumea, I retired to the forward cabin for my afternoon snooze. It had been two days since I had had the pleasure.

We were greeted by the usual officials and, an hour later, by a reporter. It was about time the press took notice of *Molly Brown* and her gallant crew. While the reporter set up his tape recorder, I braced myself for the interview. Once the machine was going, he turned not to me but to Maryrose and began asking questions, which she gleefully answered. The conversation was in French, of course. The reporter was from the local radio station, and the topic of the interview ran along the lines of how a French cook faced life on the bounding main. Well, that's show biz.

The Maryrose Show completed, we motored to the yacht club, something I had forgotten existed. There was even a gas pump on the dock. And slips for boats. For the first time since leaving U.S. waters, I was not going to have to tote fuel in jerry jugs or pump up the rubber boat. We pulled into a slip and tied up alongside a Tahiti ketch, *Schnoupi.* Her crew—a family named Jourdan—was French, which made Maryrose feel right at home. While they chatted, I thought how good it would be to get to Australia. There, at least, I could sit down at a bar with those dusty cowboys and speak American. The Jourdans, in their forties, were growing old circumnavigating. They had been out for more than four years, and planned to stay in Noumea for the school year. Typical yachties, they would rather do anything than put to sea. I would almost bet they're still in Noumea. They had a daughter, about 18, who was attractive; but most girls that age are if they're ever going to be. A son, several years younger, seemed to be the only one in the family interested in boats. He taught Maryrose how to make baggywrinkle the next day. Made by knotting frayed pieces of hemp on a line so that it resembles Christmas-tree rope, the stuff is used in rigging to prevent chafing. I don't like the looks of it; but something had to be done to save my mainsail from coming apart at the seams.

We spent three days in Noumea, roughly equivalent to a long weekend in Pittsburgh. Bauxite refineries were going full blast, the harbor was crowded with ships awaiting their turn at conveyors, and all the shops were busy. It wasn't pretty, but it was progress.

Back on the pier at the yacht club, Jack Owens put out his large sunburned arm to shake hands. Tugboat captain and unofficial welcoming committee to foreign yachts, he asked if I would be kind enough to deliver a package to Australia. The package, he explained, contained an engine part for the yacht *La Salle,* which had left Noumea a week ago. I promised Jack the mail would go through. After that he bought me a drink, recommended that I dump a little graphite into the crankcase to free a sticking valve, and drove me to the weather station to check on any severe lows between here and Australia. There were none, although that situation could change without much notice, for this was the time of year that hurricanes began winding up in these latitudes. The odds were pretty much in our favor, as the pilot charts showed an average of one storm a month in this area. Now I am not one to advocate taking risks at sea; but considering the vast area involved, the relative movements of vessel and storm, and early warnings via radio, chances are good that you can stay out of trouble. Besides, hurricane or no, the ocean is a hell of a lot safer on a Saturday night than some places I've been. I decided we would leave in the morning. That evening we had a party on the pier. The old barbecue, though badly corroded, still had a couple of fires left in her. The Jourdans brought wine, Jack made a salad, and I cooked steaks backyard style.

Despite my desire to leave early—so that we would have ample sunlight to get through Dumbea Pass—it was 11 A.M. before we motored out of the harbor. Jack had cautioned me about the coral but not the sun, which by mid-afternoon was right in my eyes. I couldn't see a damned thing. Slowing *Molly Brown* to a near idle, we poked along waiting for sunset or, better yet, a nice cloud cover. The keel bumped the first time at five o'clock. It was solid coral, and I winced as we scraped over it. By six the sun had lost some of its brightness, and visibility improved. Then wham! The boat bumped hard again, shaking the hell out of the rigging. I threw the helm over and turned 180 degrees. Back on the coral we crunched. Now what should I do? I sure as hell couldn't anchor here. And with no overhead sun to show the depth of the water, I didn't dare try getting out. Even if I had, it would have meant returning to Nouméa in the dark—suicide in this spooky pass.

Pure lovely luck—you just can't beat it. A returning fishing boat saw us and led us out of the jungle. By nine o'clock we had cleared the reef and were back in the Pacific trades with headsails set. In front of us stretched 900 miles of open water.

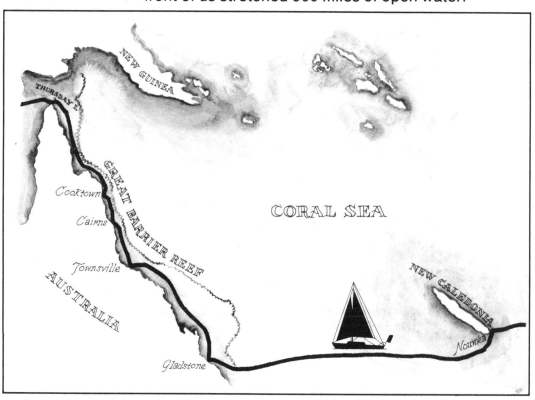

Chapter 8

**Sunday,
November 9:**

Clear, sunny, beautiful day. Lovely sailing in a force three southeast breeze. For dinner we feast on steak with Béarnaise sauce, cauliflower, and roast potatoes. It's obvious we are not long out of port.

**Monday,
November 10:**

After breakfast, Maryrose starts making baggywrinkle. She has the stuff running in two strands from the forward cabin all the way back through the main cabin, which pretty well eliminates the possibility of me doing anything below. I get my clipboard, go topside, and write a letter to my sister Sallie. After dinner it starts raining, gently at first, then it turns into a real frog strangler. At midnight I brush the baggywrinkle off my bunk and am lulled to sleep by the sound of rain spattering on a fiberglass roof.

**Tuesday,
November 11:**

Still raining hard. We are progressively getting more southing, which means deteriorating weather conditions. A noon latitude, with just a glimpse of the sun, puts us 22 degrees, 10 minutes south, but that's as much a guess as anything. The wind is fluky and around the compass all day.

**Wednesday,
November 12:**

Clearing in the morning, with the wind backing to the northeast—a fair breeze. My back is aching; has been since I lifted the heavy plow anchor back in Tonga. Maryrose says roll over and she'll fix me up. She bought a bottle of some sort of horse liniment in Caledonia and rubs it in with gusto. I believe it is boiled snake fat. Anyway, it seems to help. I ask her if she would like a rubdown, and she says not now.

Thursday, November 13: A noon fix puts us 345 miles from Lady Elliot light, the entrance I have chosen on the Great Barrier Reef. After lunch of sardines and one of Maryrose's seagoing salads—sliced onions, beets, and canned peas pickled in vinegar—she turns on the radio in hopes of picking up a little Australian music. The powerful voice of Radio Brisbane booms in. We listen to the news and learn that the world is still screwed up. That afternoon I write letters, reminding family and friends of what I promised before I left Annapolis—that I would be in Australia for Thanksgiving. They said I would never make it. If we don't make it now, it will be because we pile up on the rocks.

Friday, November 14: The wind honks up through the night, and it's raining again. A sun line, shot under unfavorable conditions, puts us about 23° south latitude. Squalls pepper us all afternoon and evening. I cannot get a star fix, but would dead reckon we're about 200 miles east of Curtis Channel, marked on the north by Lady Elliot light and on the south by Fraser Island light. The entrance is 25 miles wide, which even I should be able to hit.

Saturday, November 15: Conditions still bad, with thunderstorms and squalls. Maryrose is seasick. I make her some hot tea, but I doubt that she can keep it down. Skies clear for awhile in the evening, and I get a celestial fix. We're 80 miles out of Lady Elliot.

The log says "bad squall," but that's an understatement for what hit us at three the next morning. The first bolt of lightning was so close that I thought it had struck the boat. I was out of the sack and on deck before the flash faded. Knowing we were going to get clobbered in a matter of seconds, I set the vane right into the wind, then yanked the working jib down and lashed it temporarily to the pulpit. When I pulled the brake on the main halyard winch, boom and sail crashed into the cockpit, narrowly missing Maryrose standing there in foul-weather gear. By now it was blowing a good 60 knots, but this was no time for a breather. I tied some line around the headsail and lashed the main to the fallen boom. The entire job took only about 15 minutes, although it seemed like hours. But, wouldn't you know it? Once I had finished, the squall blew out, and there wasn't a breath of air. The sea was still choppy as hell, though.

It had cleared enough by noon for a sun shot, which showed us to be due east of Curtis Pass. That afternoon Radio Brisbane was alerting one and all to the violent squalls that were moving along the coast blowing off roofs and knocking down barns—and, we could have added, pounding the daylights out of little sailboats. In the evening I shot Vega, Rigil Kent, and Arcturus, and picked up a beacon on the RDF. I sat in the cockpit until 11 P.M. looking for the flash from Lady Elliot or Breaksea Spit. As I could see neither, I figured we must be smack in the middle of the pass. I turned on the masthead light—so traffic could steer clear of us—and went below for a snooze. Back on deck at 2 A.M., I saw the flash from Bustard Head over the starboard bow. This meant we were well within the Barrier Reef, as the light had a range of 24 miles and was on the mainland to the north of us. I went below for another nap, setting my alarm clock for five. I got up with the sun, and there it was—the east coast of Australia, high, barren, and beautiful. I could have swum ashore and kissed it.

Although, from all appearances, my navigating was spot on, I decided to check it anyway. I got a noon line and plotted it. Longitude and latitude crossed two miles northeast of Bustard Head—exactly where we were. On to Gladstone! I cracked sheets and we bore off along the beach. After awhile it dawned on me that our chart of this section of the Barrier Reef didn't describe how to get into Port Curtis, the harbor of Gladstone. Just before dark I motored toward shore and asked a fellow on an ore-loading dock where the yachts anchored in Gladstone. "Go to the next white flasher and swing hard to port," he yelled. I thanked him, and off we went, Maryrose at the helm. An hour later we rounded a bend and saw the white flasher. "Which side do we go on?" Maryrose asked. "Swing hard to the left as soon as you pass the mark," I guessed. She did, and *Molly Brown* came to an abrupt halt, her keel buried deep in Australian mud. It is distressing to travel 10,000 miles, then get stuck in the mud. After dinner I dozed off, only to be awakened by the movement of the boat a little after midnight. The tide had come in, and *Molly Brown* was once again afloat. I hit the starter, the old Universal picked up on three out of four cylinders, and we proceeded to the concrete quay, where we tied up for the remainder of the night.

While Maryrose heated coffee, I got the flags up, then took a stroll around the quay to see how it felt to be walking on the opposite side of the earth. When I returned, the boat was filled with fishermen and cattlemen sipping coffee. Maryrose was holding open house before we had officially entered the country. That, as I experienced later in the morning, was a simple matter of filling out ten long and complicated forms. It couldn't have been worse had *Molly Brown* been a Polaris submarine.

A small mining town, Gladstone sits on a big hill, with the post office, bank, and hotel all near the top. We walked up the dusty hill to the post office and, sure enough, there was a letter from my brother, Billy. It was now about 2 P.M., Tuesday, November 18. If I could get a call through to Billy, it would be five o'clock Monday morning, Annapolis time, which is not a bad hour to be getting up for a farm boy. In ten minutes he was on the line. We chatted rapidly—at five bucks a minute a southern drawl can be costly—assuring each other that things were okay on our respective sides of the world. Most encouraging was the news that he had a lucrative contract on some land I had a third interest in. The figures sounded too good to be true, and I assumed the deal would never go to settlement. But if it did, it would make both me and the IRS very happy. Buoyed by the promise of riches, after I hung up I told Maryrose that I would buy her the best lunch in Gladstone. And I did. A beer and an eggburger. An eggburger, if you've never tried one, is fried egg and hamburger in a roll with a slice of tomato. Maryrose and I had two each and I don't know how many nickel glasses of beer.

We returned to *Molly Brown,* where a convention was in progress. The consensus of opinion of the local gentry was that Townsville, about 500 miles up the coast, offered more amenities to visiting yachtsmen than a mining town like Gladstone. For one thing, if the boat needed repairs—which it did—they could be done there but not here. There was agreement all around on that point but not on the next—my plan to sail all the way up the reef and across the Arafura Sea to Darwin. By Christmas. "Son," counseled a wiry old man who had spent most of his life piloting boats on the reef, "you will never make it up the reef now. Lay over in Townsville for the winter and leave early in the spring. The hurricane season will be over then, the tides will be more favorable, and you will have a fair breeze." This was not what I hoped to hear, so I moved on to a new source—two cowboys (or ringers, as they are called here) standing on the dock, their hats thrown back and dust covering their Levis. Normally one would not request nautical information from cowhands, but these were a breed unto themselves. I had watched them as they tied their wooden barge to the quay. Their business was trading cattle up and down the reef. The fellow who appeared to be the captain or trail boss, as the case might be, said: "You got an engine in that thing, don't you? What bloody difference does it make where the wind comes from?" I had found a very knowledgeable Australian.

The third person I talked to on the quay was Eric Kraak, who owned an old but well-maintained Tahiti ketch named *Tangari.* He and his cook, Jean, planned to leave that afternoon, and invited us to sail with them. I thought that was a splendid idea. After Maryrose retrieved our clothes, still damp, from the local coin-operated laundry and I filled our gas cans, the two boats departed at 5 P.M. Motoring out of Gladstone behind Eric, I found it hard to believe we weren't coasting down the Intercoastal Waterway in Georgia. Curtis Island on one side, miles of marsh on the other; clumps of trees here and there with branches bending into the stream; hogs standing knee-deep in mud; debris floating down water so black and thick it all but stuck to the sides of the boat; the heat and the humidity; the mosquitoes. No wonder I got a little homesick for the South. At eight o'clock Eric flagged me over and suggested we stop for the night. I dropped my fenders and we tied up to his anchor. Jean fixed dinner, which was served aboard *Tangari.* Feeling either guilty or jealous that she wasn't in the kitchen, Maryrose announced that breakfast for all hands would be dished up on *Molly Brown* at 6:30 sharp in the morning. Eric and Jean showed up on time and even stayed for lunch, which we ate on the run, *Molly Brown* towing the ketch. Eric had made many trips up and down the reef, but he had never been to sea. And he had no desire to go. As he explained: "A well-built boat to explore the reef, a well-built cook to keep me company, why leave?" I had no answer.

After he and Jean returned to their ketch, Maryrose put out about 300 feet of fishing line. The longer the line, the bigger the fish, she figured. It would take a huge fish to swallow the huge hook she was trailing. That afternoon a freshly painted yacht approached from the north. Eric recognized the captain as Pelorus Jack, a legend on the reef and, more than that, a character in Australian folklore. Eric had told me about him the night before in terms reminiscent of old Mississippi River keelboatmen. Pelorus Jack, he said, was born on a coral head, raised by a school of porpoises, and spent his days cruising the reef and playing a piano. The piano, Eric explained with a straight face, was in the main cabin. It was a good yarn, but I didn't believe for a minute that there was any such person as Pelorus Jack. Even now I was wondering if Eric was putting me on. If so, it was a damned good acting job, for he was advancing his throttle and racing out to greet the old man. And I heard him call his name—Pelorus Jack. Anxious to meet this living legend, I slowed *Molly Brown* and circled alongside. Too late I remembered Maryrose's fishing line. In coming around I pulled the hook all the way down Pelorus Jack's boat, ruining the new paint job. I retrieved the line, then swung alongside and yelled an apology. Pelorus Jack never heard me. He had gone below to play his piano.

We said goodbye to Eric and Jean and headed for our first night in the Barrier Reef. As soon as I had hoisted the main and genoa, Maryrose put that long fishing line back into the water. A few minutes later she hauled in a dolphin that filled the cockpit. She said that if I would fillet it, she would "ceviche" it. Ceviching, she explained, is a South American way of pickling fish she had learned in the Galapagos. It involves soaking the fish overnight in vinegar with onions and an assortment of spices. It will keep two or three days that way, and is very tasty—far better than raw. About midnight we collided with a bad squall, with nonstop lightning. That was scary but not all bad, for it illuminated the obstructions around us as well as magnified them. I took down the sails, and we lay there all night.

Using a chart purchased in Panama as a road map, we set out the next morning for Middle Island. Blessed with a fine beach, a cool stream, and no people, it was an ideal place to enjoy a picnic and a nap. As we lay contentedly on my old army blanket, I wondered why such a beautiful island was deserted. Suddenly I heard the answer in a throaty howl. A wolflike dog, its ears laid back, was coming our way. We grabbed the blanket and raced to the boat a couple of pants ahead of the dog. I hauled out the chart and picked another island—Whitsunday, 110 miles up the coast. It was a tourist resort, and presumably all the dogs there were on leashes. Pushed by a fair easterly that soon built into a strong easterly—force six, at least—we shot up the channel. I did the piloting, Maryrose the steering. Though we were in relatively open water, it was all she could do to control the boat. My chart showed a 30-mile patch of coral heads, reefs, and islands ahead, which I estimated we would reach about midnight. By the time we got to the first obstruction, Bailey Reef, marked by a flasher, the wind was blowing at nearly gale strength. With sail reduced to a storm jib, we entered the pass at the reef. There was little else we could do, certainly not turn back in that wind. Neither could we anchor in 30 fathoms of water. As for heaving to, I felt that unwise with so many obstructions around. Still, if we had hit anything at our speed—about five knots—*Molly Brown,* without a doubt, would have gone to the bottom. I wasn't too worried about that happening, for I had worked out the proper compass course, and we were following it. At least we were until a thunderstorm rolled in about 1 A.M. As on the night before, I dropped the headsail and watched the lightning silhouette batteries of rocks waiting to grab us. If we can make it through till dawn, I vowed, I'll never try a midnight ride like that again.

Bright sun and hot coffee made a world of difference. Now the task was to pilot past the rest of the obstacles and on to Whitsunday. As I stood on deck surveying the bewildering array of islands and coral reefs ahead, I asked Maryrose to hand up the chart so I could figure out a way through them. She did, and the wind blew it right out of my hands.

It is possible to navigate through that particular area without a chart, for we did it. It is also possible for a participant to play Russian roulette without blowing his head off.

Whitsunday was a pain in the ass. The only friendly person we encountered was the bartender, who smiled every time we ordered another drink. We did look a bit unpressed, but that was no reason to shun us. Hell, for all these people knew, I might have been Howard Hughes traveling incognito and ready to pass out thousand dollar bills to anyone who said hello. Meandog island was a much friendlier place. A night's sleep, another rubdown with Maryrose's magic liniment, and we were off for Townsville, 130 miles up the reef.

It was a pleasant passage through a lovely area, with storybook islands looming at every turn. We sailed through the night—a dry one, for a change—

without a crisis. I awoke to the sound of Johnny Cash singing "A Boy Named Sue." Maryrose had tuned in Townsville while preparing breakfast. That evening as we motored up the canal, I hoisted the Australian courtesy flag in the rigging and the American ensign high on the wind vane. I threw the dock lines to half a dozen Aussies standing on the quay, watching us come in. Welcome to Townsville, they said, and hurry; the pub closes in an hour.

Largest city on the Barrier Reef with a population of 60,000, Townsville was the obvious place to overhaul *Molly Brown* for the long jaunt across the Indian Ocean. During the five days we were there, I had her sails restitched and her valves ground. That business, coupled with resupplying and refueling the boat, left little time for sightseeing, though—thanks to a $1,000 check from Billy waiting for me at the post office—I did accomplish a bit of Christmas shopping for my children. Unable to buy a live kangaroo and ship it home, I settled for a stuffed koala, a boomerang, and some other things the kids down the block wouldn't likely get. Late Wednesday evening, November 26 (Thanksgiving morning in the States), I called home. My son, Richard, answered the phone:

"Hello."

"Hi, Richard. How are you?"

"Fine, Daddy."

"What are you doing?"

"Nothing."

"How is Kyle?"

"She's in the hospital."

"What?"

"Uncle Lory took her to the hospital."

"For God's sake, Richard, let me speak to Aunt Sallie."

Boy, was I shook up for a second. I was within an ace of racing to the airport and catching the first plane out. My sister, with a cheery hello, soon put my mind at ease. Kyle, she assured me, was okay. She had gashed her leg on a barbed wire fence and needed a couple of stitches. After hearing that, I loosened up and talked forty dollars' worth to everyone there—from my father on down the line.

While in Townsville, I met Lindsey Buckmaster, a delightful chap from Melbourne. He was about 25, wore a dense black beard, and had a fine sense of humor. Being co-owner—and builder—of a trimaran, he was also a knowledgeable sailor. I asked him if he would like to take a busman's holiday aboard *Molly Brown*. Since he was unemployed at the time, he signed on for as far as Darwin. Maryrose, figuring that with an extra hand she wouldn't have to stand watch so much, gave enthusiastic approval. Before we shoved off, a newspaper reporter dropped by and requested an interview. With me. That was more like it. He mentioned that we were the second American yacht to visit Townsville in a fortnight. *La Salle* had left the week before.

At 3 P.M. on Monday, December 1, we sailed. Our track would be all the way to the top of the reef, then westward through Torres Strait and across the Arafura Sea to Darwin, a distance of 1200 miles. I promised we would be in Darwin for Christmas dinner. Our first stop was Cairns, unscheduled but a necessity since we had been motoring for two days—and the reef is no place to get caught with dry tanks. On the evening of the third we motored into the harbor and, finding no space at the quay, headed for a cluster of boats. Maybe somebody there could tell us where we could anchor. We swung alongside a boat lit by a kerosene lantern. In the cockpit sat a shapely blond clad only in the bottom half of a bikini. She asked what we wanted. While Lindsey and I struggled for the proper words to address this Lady Godiva, Maryrose smiled and told her we were looking for a place to park. "Why not beside us?" came the husky reply. Overboard went the fenders, splash went the anchor, and below went the blond. She returned with the rest of her bikini and Phil, her husband. We invited them over for a drink and small talk. Phil was skeptical that a glass boat could make it through the reef. If you hit a piece of coral, he said, she will crack open like an egg. Phil was a newspaperman and obviously knew a lot about boats. Suzy, the blond, made bikinis, and, I presume, modeled them. Both were vegetarians; but, hell, I am too at times—especially when *Molly Brown* runs low on provisions. We got gas the next day and some more of that good nickel beer. Early the following morning we were back in the channel going for Cooktown, 90 miles up the coast.

It was smooth sailing all day, and by 11 P.M. we were off Thomas Point, only 15 miles south of Cooktown. Then came the rain and trouble. Lindsey spotted the range lights of a ship bearing down on us and asked me if we should change course. I didn't think so, assuming that with our present heading we would cross the ship's bow and pass starboard to starboard. A few minutes later the throb of engines and blast of a horn told me I was wrong. We were on a collision course. I swung hard to port, which was stupid, because now we were laying broadside to the ship and in imminent danger of being sliced in half. Fortunately, the rain slacked, the ship backed down, and *Molly Brown* slithered by unscathed. The only excuse for pulling such a stunt was that I feared we might bang into the reef off to the right. I had a bad case of coral fever. Probing in the midnight darkness for Cooktown harbor, I ran *Molly Brown* up on the mud. But that is nothing unusual for a Chesapeake Bay sailor. The tide came in at four in the morning and we floated off. At daylight we tied up to an old wooden quay. Lindsey didn't say anything, but I could hear what he was thinking: How in the hell did we ever get this far in one piece?

Back in 1770 Capt. James Cook did what I was afraid of doing to *Molly Brown.* He drove *Endeavor* onto the rocks—and, incidentally, discovered the Great Barrier Reef. In the protected little harbor where we now stood, he limped ashore to make repairs and to leave his name upon the land. We asked two fishermen on the quay the way to town. "Follow the road, matey," one obliged, "you can't miss it." If it had been raining we could have easily missed it. But it wasn't, and from the looks of things, it hadn't all year.

A dozen frame buildings lined the dusty street. On the right stood the Cooktown Museum, admission 50 cents. We decided to find the pub first. The building with the most cars parked in front I figured to be either a whorehouse or a saloon. It was the pub. And business wasn't all that good. They even let Maryrose in, which broke the rule of men only in Aussie bars. Lindsey and I each had four quick cold ones and Maryrose three. She was sitting next to the mayor, who, with pardonable civic pride, announced that the Queen planned to visit Cooktown. The Queen of what, I wondered—Tonga? Pausing to buy an ice cream cone for his dog under the bar stool, the mayor said, "I reckon we will start to tidy up the town a bit tomorrow." I reckoned we had better be dusting along, and after another for the road, we said goodbye and headed for the boat. The beer was working on Maryrose. Stricken with a sudden craving for culture, she said she wasn't leaving town until she toured the museum. "If it's good enough for the Queen," she declared, "it's good enough for me." We plunked down 50 cents apiece and circled through. A couple of cannon balls, an old naval uniform, and a model of *Endeavor* made by the mayor was about the extent of it. At a quarter till four we were back on the boat and underway. We had spent a little money, seen everybody in town including His Honor, and visited the museum. I felt like I was born and raised in Cooktown.

We were having to stop every couple of days for fuel because I wasn't carrying any in the jerry jugs. Too risky. If you hit something in this narrow channel and one of those cans spilled gas on the deck, one spark would make the fiberglass boat look like a toasted marshmallow. We motored up to Cape Flattery and parked for the night. With the reefs closing in, I thought it wise to wait for a little sunlight, so we could see where we were going. This was a bit inconsistent with past performance, but that's why I did it—past performance. At first light we were underway, entering Portland Roads about 9 A.M. A large research vessel—*Seaboy II*—took up all the space at the pier, and I requested permission to tie alongside her—or him. The captain granted it and, after inviting us aboard, asked if we needed assistance. I told him we had come in for gas. You won't find it here, he said, for Portland Roads consisted of a single house occupied by a crazy old hermit. Then why the long pier? "You chaps put it here." During the Battle of the Coral Sea, this was a Yank airbase, he explained; but the place had been deserted since the end of the war. *Seaboy,* engaged in mineral exploration, used the facilities to field her land crew that worked in the bush, with the airfield serving as a landing pad for the ship's helicopter. The captain said that he had only diesel oil for the ship and aviation fuel for the chopper, but they might have some gas at the aborigine reserve about 30 miles inland. He would get the manager on the wireless. A few minutes later we received word that a drum of fuel would be sent out that afternoon.

We were invited to make ourselves at home, which included raiding the fridge stocked with cold beer. After Lindsey and I had a couple, we decided to explore the ghost airbase, leaving Maryrose to awe the Aussies with tales of Gay Paree and other stops on her itinerary. We walked the length of the long, wooden quay, past Crazy Charley's hut, and up the abandoned road to the weed-covered airstrip. Rusting gasoline drums and skeletons of trucks, World War II vintage, littered the underbrush. Buffeted by hot wind, we stood on the airfield and looked out to the razor-edge horizon, a scene not too dissimilar to the ocean when calm. If for a minute it seemed changeless, that was suddenly shattered by a trail of billowing dust followed by a thundering roar. Was it a crippled B-24 coming in for a belly landing? When the cloud of dust finally cleared, we saw three heavy trucks, one with a large reefer filled with beer, the other two with drilling equipment and half a dozen Aussies coming in from the bush for a four-day furlough on *Seaboy.* They were drunk and bent on getting drunker. I feared for Maryrose's virginity. Needlessly, it turned out. Not one of the young drillers laid a paw on her. But this might have been because every hand was wrapped around a can of beer.

It was after midnight when we returned to *Molly Brown.* Perhaps emboldened by the alcohol in our veins—as well as charts of the reef the captain gave us and a full tank of gas—we sailed forthwith. But God watches over drunks and little children. We didn't hit a thing.

In mid-afternoon we pulled over to Hannibal Reef for a rest stop. With its lone palm tree, it looked like a cartoon. After spending five minutes exploring every inch of the islet, we retired to the beach. There was considerable shipping, so we didn't pay much attention to the large vessel anchored a mile or so off the island. But we did take notice when its launch headed toward us. My first thought was that we must be trespassing on someone's private property and were about to get thrown off. Expect the worst and you'll find the worst. Not so this time. The smartly turned out sailor in the launch came with an invitation: Capt. Phil Brooke of the Royal Australian Navy survey vessel *Palouma* requested the pleasure of our company for dinner. We said we'd be delighted, shook the sand out of our shoes, and hied over in *Molly Brown.* We made her fast and scrambled up the rope ladder. Immaculate in navy whites and trimmed black beard, Capt. Brooke was waiting with outstretched hand. Over cocktails in the wardroom, we were soon on a first-name basis. Phil inquired about our voyage and explained the mission of his ship—to chart the ever-changing reef. Dinner was fine Australian beef followed by brandy and a political discussion. Phil thought President Johnson was a perfect fool to get us so heavily committed in Southeast Asia. I said, well, if he wasn't a horse's ass, he would not have been in politics in the first place. With the brandy doing wonders for my brain, I went on to say that it was a damned shame we had ever separated from the Crown. Phil looked surprised and said, "Really, old chap." "Yes," I continued, "I would far rather have my destiny in the hands of a properly educated king or queen than some Mickey Mouse politician with his hand in my pocket." We passed the brandy a few more times and parted good friends at 2 A.M.

With Lindsey and I taking turns at the helm, we rode the flood tide into Thursday Island about four in the afternoon. The Great Barrier Reef was behind us, and open water lay ahead. Eager to get back to sea, I announced that Thursday Island would be little more than a pit stop.

We climbed the hill to the Grandview hotel, a pink three-story structure with a widow's walk around the roof. A large center hall divided the Grandview. On the left, behind the front porch, was an antiquated sitting room where two antiquated ladies were having tea. Diagonally across the hall was the main dining room, its faded drapes moving lightly in the breeze. Half a dozen elderly couples, dining in funereal silence, didn't bother to look up as we were shown to our table. Feeling a little out of place in these sedate surroundings, we hurried through the meal, keeping our voices low and our elbows off the table. As we walked back into the main hall, Lindsey noticed a bar sign on a massive closed door opposite the dining room. How we missed it the first time I do not know. I leaned against the heavy door and was met by a roar of voices and a whistling dart. I was right in the line of fire of a game between a gigantic aborigine and a well-dressed Chinese. They suspended action long enough for us to cross to the long wooden bar crowded with sweaty men of assorted nationalities. Everybody was drinking beer and talking at the top of their lungs, a large improvement, I thought, over the dining room crowd. The action soon shifted to one corner of the room, where an argument flared between an Indian and an aborigine. The blonde proprietress of the Grandview, her tremendous busts forming a spearhead, dashed to the trouble spot and evicted the troublemakers without one word being raised in protest. The customers seemed to have great respect for their Miss Kitty of Thursday Island, otherwise known as Thirsty Island.

We spent the next day taking on provisions and gasoline for the 800-mile run across the Arafura Sea. I was not expecting a pleasant passage. If the pilot charts were right, as they usually were, we would be bucking strong headwinds much of the way to Darwin.

We cleared customs Saturday morning, December 13, and motored past an Australian gunboat tied to the quay. *Attack* was written across her stern and three sets of glasses in the wheelhouse were trained on *Molly Brown*—or, more specifically, Maryrose. Always the lady, she responded by sticking out her tongue. With lots of sun and no air, we put up the awning and headed west.

For five days we motored, not an unpleasant way to travel if you have an extra hundred gallons of gasoline. Unfortunately, we didn't; the jerry cans were now empty, and the bottom of the tank was visible. Also visible was Cape Wessel, off the port bow. "Captain," said Lindsey, "there is no sense flopping out here. Let's go play on the beach till a breeze comes in." We loaded the Avon with sandwiches, towels, camera, and whatever else an explorer of note might need and paddled for the deserted shore. It was a lovely place, known only to God and perhaps a wandering aborigine; but for now, ours were the only footprints in the sand. At sundown a breeze rippled our canopy of palm fronds. "Lindsey," I said, "Darwin is calling."

It took us six days to sail the remaining 400 miles to Darwin. The wind jumped around the compass like a flea on a hot grill, never remaining constant in speed or direction for more than a couple of hours. When it did attempt to settle down in earnest, a black squall as mean as a baby tornado would come cruising in off the horizon. For Monday, December 22, the third successive day of stormy weather, I entered in the log: "Heavy squalls all night and morning. Miserable sailing." That evening, however, conditions improved, and the next afternoon we charged into Darwin under full sail.

We dropped the hook beside *La Salle.* For four months we had chased her and her crew across the South Pacific. It was time we got acquainted. "Hi, Hal!" I yelled to the middle-aged fellow standing on deck. "What in hell are you doing way out here with

Sally and the kids?" His mouth dropped open, but no words came out. A few minutes later the formalities were out of the way and we were rapping like old buddies who hadn't seen each other since way back when. The Autenreiths were leaving for Bali tomorrow. They had been out for more than a year and were determined to be back in the States by fall, in time for the four children, ages seven through 15, to start to school. I gave Hal the engine part I had been hauling for several thousand miles and invited the family to Christmas Eve dinner on *Molly Brown.*

Lindsey and I then went in to check with port authorities before the offices closed. We paddled to the steel quay, tied the Avon to the lowest landing (the tide was out), and walked up the stairs and into town. We arrived at customs just as the office Christmas party was getting under way. We had a choice of leaving without getting cleared or joining the party and taking care of business afterwards. We chose the latter. Three hours later we headed back to the quay, stopping on the way to buy some steaks. "Lindsey," I said, "things don't look the same. Are you sure we're in the right port?" He thought a minute and said we were, because he could see *Molly Brown* and *La Salle.* What we couldn't see were the steps and the Avon. Finally we figured out that the tide had come in, covering the securely lashed rubber boat with 18 feet of water. We hitched a ride in a rowboat and delivered the goods without further mishap.

Christmas morning Jimmy, Eric, Archie, and Wendy Autenreith sailed over in their Dyer dink to wish us a Merry Christmas. We watched them return to *La Salle* and pull the dinghy aboard. Hal already had the mainsail up, and it was luffing in a freshening breeze. Jimmy hoisted the large overlapping genoa, and Archie cast the mooring line free. Her sheets trimmed, *La Salle* gathered momentum. When she came by, her crew was waving, and she was driving for Bali.

Lindsey, Maryrose, and I went to the Oceanal restaurant for Christmas dinner. Turkey wasn't on the menu, so we settled for filet mignon with mushroom sauce and a bottle of Burgundy. Back on the boat we exchanged small gifts, Maryrose presenting me with a pair of sunglasses that I lost next day in the harbor. They fell out of my pocket when Lindsey and I were tying *Molly Brown* to an abandoned barge which served as a dry dock when the tide went out. Using Aussie ingenuity, Lindsey replaced the corroded ground plate for the radio telephone, fashioning a new one out of a brass foghorn. Then we touched up the bottom with a quart of paint before the tide rolled in. That night we took in a movie, the first flick I had seen since leaving Annapolis.

On Monday an old friend pulled into the harbor. It was *Attack,* her guns bristling. "Maryrose," I said, "you're in a world of trouble. They've found you." *Attack* and her sister ship, *Jaguar,* were taking Christmas leave in Darwin, not the liveliest town for a sailor to raise hell in—which is probably why the brass sends them here. We got to know the crews when scouting for gas; they invited us aboard for cold beer. I can't imagine the men on an American gunboat doing a thing like that. It's probably a court-martial offense. We may rule the waves; but those Aussies— they waive the rules.

Tuesday was our last day in Darwin. And like all last days in port, we were busy stowing things and getting ready to sail. At sea you don't turn back if you forget your toothbrush. I called home and talked to my kids, which should have made me happy; but this time of year it was tough not seeing the happy faces around the Christmas tree. I even missed the snow and ice. Maryrose said I was homesick; and I said, you're probably right. Let's saddle up. Lindsey had obtained a job in Darwin as a cabinetmaker and was going to stay awhile. He walked with us to the boat after a farewell dinner in a Greek restaurant. Before he left, I asked him to sign the logbook, and he did, adding: "Hope the trip continues as it has been."

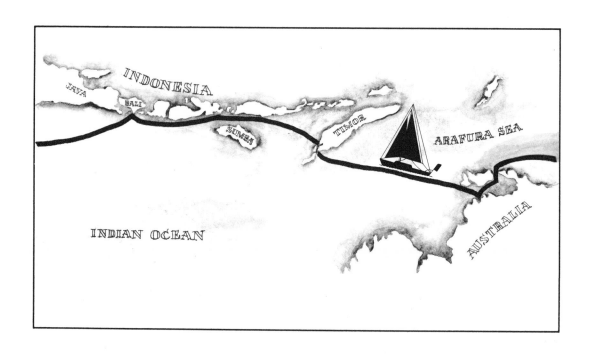

Chapter 9

Wednesday, December 31:   Bali bound! We wave goodbye to *Attack* and motor out of the harbor at 1500. Four hours later I hoist the main and genny and tack into a force three westerly. At 2400 the sea is calm, the night warm and clear and deathly quiet. The only sound comes from the forward cabin, where Maryrose is softly snoring. I close the door, pour myself a Scotch, take it up on deck and stand there looking into the velvety black night.

Thursday, January 1, 1970:   The wind comes in from the north, slowly backs to the west, and freshens. By breakfast time, it is blowing at force four and *Molly Brown* is pounding. I reef the main. A noon sun line shows we're way too far north. After sundown, the wind moderates, and I try for more westing.

Friday, January 2:   I tack back and forth all morning in fluky air, but a sun shot at 1300 tells me we are not getting as much westing as we need. We motor awhile to improve our heading, then go back to canvas—main and No. 1 genny. At 2000 the wind is west-southwest at force two, and I'm tired. It's all yours, self-steerer.

Saturday, January 3:	Rain blowing in an open port awakens me at 0500. I drop No. 1 and go back to bed. I can't sleep. The squall passes, and I get up and make a pot of coffee, then go up on deck and wait for the sun. It peeps over the edge of the water like a big jack-o-lantern. At noon I tack. At 1730 we're becalmed. I start the engine and motor for an hour.
Sunday, January 4:	We almost have company for breakfast. Maryrose hooks a small shark, but it breaks the tackle as she's hoisting it over the side. A favorable breeze in the afternoon boosts our speed to four knots, but we are still running too far north. After dinner we sit on the cabin top and watch lightning flash in the west.
Monday, January 5:	A small squall rocks us at 0200, but hardly enough to get out of bed for. Daybreak finds us becalmed. I top the tank with ten gallons out of the cans, crank the engine, and start motoring. At 0800 we sight the mountains of Timor. A noon sun line tells me we are about 100 miles north of the lower end of the island, which means we are 100 miles off course to Bali. We motor and sail down the coast, Maryrose and I standing four-hour watches.
Tuesday, January 6:	At 0600 I take over in a glassy sea. Back to power. Maryrose, sounding a lot like John Tucker, says she would rather fish than sleep and proceeds to catch a tuna. We enter Roti passage in late afternoon and motor up Semau pass toward Kupang, on the opposite side of the island. It's dark when we drop the hook outside a fishing village. There are about a dozen work boats anchored nearby, most of them about 40 feet long. Families evidently live on them, for we see cooking fires going on deck and a lot of kids. A small trading ship is tied at the quay, where about 50 dark-skinned men are unloading her. A loudspeaker system going full blast entertains them with music, and I recognize the tune. Elvis Presley singing "You Ain't Nothin' but a Hound Dog."

Next morning we breakfasted on fried eggs, rice, and the tuna Maryrose caught; then we weighed anchor and motored to the quay. The trading ship having left in the night, we were spared an encore by Elvis. I was a little uneasy about going ashore, since we had no clearance papers for Indonesian waters. But if this was Kupang, Timor's major port, maybe I could talk officials into granting us a visa. Friendly men on the dock told us we were five miles south of Kupang. However, a smiling fellow in a straw hat offered to call the immigration office to see if someone could come down and take care of us. Fortunately, the only telephone in the village was on the dock, and the call didn't take but a minute. We were told to motor up to Kupang.

It was a nice ride along the coast, a ribbon of rock broken by patches of green. Squat grass-roofed huts crowded right up to the water's edge; step out the front door and you get your feet wet. In a few minutes I discovered that we were about to get *our* feet wet. The bilge had flooded, and water was coming up through the floorboards. I cut the engine and began pumping. The trouble was a blown seal on the engine's salt-water cooling pump. That didn't bother me because I had a spare seal as well as an extra pump. In Kupang I would fix it. I pumped the bilge dry and waited for a breeze. It came right on time, and in an hour we were anchored in the harbor and paddling ashore in the Avon.

A gaggle of brown-eyed, barefoot kids met us; but since none of them understood English, they couldn't tell us where to find the immigration office. We strode up the beach into the little town and stopped an Indonesian soldier dressed in olive green but without a weapon. He couldn't speak English either, but he was accommodating and, motioning us to follow, led us to the port captain's office, a small building flanked by two young soldiers who must have been all of 16 years old.

The port captain couldn't have been nicer. Speaking excellent English, he asked why we had come to Timor without an entry permit. I told him we'd had engine trouble, were taking on water, and needed to come in and get the boat repaired. I also said we would like to stay a few days and rest up. He said he didn't think this would be permitted, but he would do what he could, assuring us it was okay with him. He tried to call immigrations but couldn't get through, then scribbled a note, handed it to a guard, and directed him to drive us to the customs and immigration building. After that things turned slightly bureaucratic.

Immigrations didn't want to be responsible for us. Neither did customs. Nor the police. We waited all afternoon while pompous officials yelled into telephones. Finally the immigrations officer called us in and demanded to know where we had cleared from and where we were bound. I said Darwin and Bali. He said we couldn't stay in Indonesia and would have to go back to Darwin. I got a little upset, to the amusement of Maryrose, and told him he could not order us back to Darwin; then I suggested where he could go. He sputtered and picked up the telephone. Maryrose and I walked out. Let's get something to eat before they throw us in jail, I said.

We found a quaint little Indian restaurant perched on a cliff overlooking the ocean. It was an informal place, a home that took in diners. A steady stream of kids bounded across the stone floor and, after we were seated, a couple of pigs walked in through the open door and lay down under the table. Fat oinking pigs, not dogs. I ate my goat meat and fried rice and drank my beer in silence. Maryrose giggled. She thought the pigs were cute.

We stayed on the boat that night, part of which I spent repairing the damned pump. Then, in the morning, back to the customs house and another round of red tape. By this time the air force and the navy had been called in, which I thought was kind of funny because there wasn't a military plane on the island or a naval vessel in the harbor. If it came to war, I had a boat and a shotgun, which was more than they had. Of course, we were outmanned. So, using diplomacy instead of a show of force, I told my story another dozen times while officials screamed at each other on the telephone. When the phone wouldn't work, which was almost 100 percent of the time, they would slam down the receiver, stamp their feet, open a window, and yell. Since everybody concerned worked in the same building, the telephone really wasn't necessary.

The air force colonel, a nervous little guy, didn't know what to do, and the indecision raged on another couple of hours. Finally, at noon, we were told we would have to leave and that we couldn't have clearance to Bali. But the officials would like to inspect our boat before we left. I said fine, right after I say goodbye to the nice port captain.

He shook his head and laughed when I told him what we had been through. Where are you going? he asked. I said it would have to be Cocos since we couldn't get clearance to Bali. He winked and said we might run out of fresh water or have engine problems when we neared Bali. And if that happened, here's the name of the port captain, a good friend and a man of great understanding. I folded the paper into my shirt pocket and shook his hand.

The air force colonel, a naval officer, and several other officials were waiting for us at the beach. Since the navy didn't have transportation, I hired a fishing boat to take them out to *Molly Brown,*

Maryrose and I taking the Avon. It was not much of an inspection, but their curiosity was satisifed, and they soon left, declining drinks I offered. The sun being over the yardarm, I poured myself one. Bali was 600 miles away, and we had enough gas to motor halfway there. At three o'clock in the afternoon, I used some of it to get us out of the harbor.

Friday, January 9: We are in the middle of the Savu Sea and still under power. We haven't felt a breeze since leaving Kupang. It is miserably hot. Up goes the awning, which helps a little. Maryrose goes to bed early; she'll take the midnight watch.

Saturday, January 10: I relieve Maryrose at 0300 and motor till 0500. Then I stop the engine and sleep for two hours. At 0930 we round the southeastern tip of Sumba. We motor all day, until the water pump conks out again. I take it apart, replace two seals, and we're off again. After dinner we drift for the night, since we're running low on fuel. I try to raise *La Salle.* No answer.

Sunday, January 11: 0800 and still becalmed. An hour later I hoist the main and genny to catch a southwest breeze. It dies in half an hour. Back to power until 1600, when we get a little air out of the south. I make the best of it as we are down to 15 gallons of fuel.

Monday, January 12: Squalls throughout the night and back in the doldrums at dawn. A noon fix puts us 205 miles out of Bali. We motor until 1600, and that just about does it; there's a gallon of gas left in the tank. We get a light breeze, but it's slow, lazy going.

Tuesday, January 13: Becalmed most of day—punk for sailing but great for swimming. So we take a swim. A light southerly springs up at 1500 and lasts for seven hours, pushing us maybe 15 miles.

Wednesday, January 14: I'm up at 0600 and feel something strange on my face—a steady breeze out of the northwest. I set the self-steerer. The breeze holds, builds to force four by noon. It moderates at dusk, dies at 2000. But I'm not complaining; this is the best sailing we've had—actually, the only sailing—since leaving port.

Thursday, January 15:

Our northwest wind returns at 0500, and I hoist the genny and main. The wind comes and goes the rest of the day, petering out for good at 2300. In the past 24 hours I've made a dozen sail changes to get 50 miles. That's working for it. But we're almost there.

Friday, January 16:

The current swept us out last night, and we're right back where we started. Fighting the current and tacking into a northwest breeze, I feel like I'm sailing a treadmill. For every two miles we gain, we lose one. I check the jugs to see if I overlooked a few drops of gas. I didn't. At dusk we approach the channel that leads into Benoa harbor. Not having a chart of the harbor, I drop the anchor beside a reef and hope we don't get a blow tonight.

I was up with the sun at six, and all around us were Balinese fishermen in brightly painted canoes. I motioned one of them to come aboard, for *Molly Brown*'s anchor was fouled on the reef, and I needed help in getting it dislodged. The bronzed young fisherman couldn't understand a word I was saying, but when I pointed down to the anchor, he grasped my meaning. He pulled on his goggles and dived into 30 feet of water. In a few seconds he had unwrapped the chain around the coral and lifted the anchor. I rewarded him with half a bottle of Scotch, which seemed to puzzle him. Evidently he had never before had a drink of whiskey, and here I was leading him astray. Maybe he took the bottle home and gave it to his old man.

With the gallon of gas I had been hoarding, we motored into the harbor. There sat *La Salle.* We spent most of the day aboard her telling the Autenreiths what had happened and trying to talk them into staying another day or two. But they said no, they were leaving in a few hours for the Seychelles and

South Africa. Perhaps we would meet again in Durban. Hal had been worried that we had run into trouble, and had alerted the captain of a Danish tanker to keep an eye out for us. If we didn't show up in a couple of days, the captain was to notify Balinese authorities. What good that would have done, I don't know. I doubt that anyone would have come looking for us.

Hal accompanied us in the dink to see the harbor master and immigration officer. In contrast to the confusion at Timor, Maryrose and I were issued visas without fuss. In an hour we were back on *La Salle* eating hard-boiled duck eggs and drinking beer. That afternoon we met Rina, a young English-speaking (more or less) Balinese of Indian ancestry who attended the college in Denpasar, Bali's capital. He had served as the Autenreith's tour guide-supplier-interpreter, a role he offered to continue with us. That was something I would have to think about, so I told him to meet me in the morning. I wasn't sure I could afford Rina. All but $70 of the thousand Billy sent me in Australia had gone for provisions, repairs, and the like; and though I had written my brother to send another thousand to Bali, I was reluctant to become a big spender until the money was in hand.

La Salle sailed at 5 P.M. Holding our parting gifts from Sally, a basket of duck eggs and a tray of ice, Maryrose and I watched the yawl motor out of the harbor. The eggs would keep but not the ice, so I put some of it in a glass with a little whiskey and silently drank to future good times with the crew of *La Salle*. Then Maryrose and I rowed ashore to the quay.

Waiting for us with a Honda 120 was Rina. Evidently he was determined to work for me whether I could pay him or not, and he was starting now, not tomorrow. After he showed me how to operate the motorbike, I took it across the causeway and back on a test run. I've got the hang of it now, I assured Rina, and he roared off on a Vespa his sister had brought down. With Maryrose on the back of the Honda, I followed him across the causeway and up the road to Denpasar, about five miles inland. We breezed past terraced rice paddies and Hindu temples into the town jammed with motorbikes, cars, trucks, and pony carts. An hour later we were sitting at the bar in the Bali Beach hotel listening to the gongs and bells of a gamelan orchestra. After dinner and a few more drinks we mounted the Honda for the ride back to *Molly Brown.* That was a mistake for two reasons: It had gotten dark and I had forgotten how to shift gears on the damned machine. A third reason might have been that I had had too much to drink, which could have accounted for the second reason. In any event, I tried, almost successfully, to sideswipe one truck and collide head-on with another on the way back to the quay. Maryrose didn't see the second truck, having closed her eyes after we passed the first.

Bali is roughly the shape of a triangle, stretching some 90 miles at the hypotenuse and 55 miles on the perpendicular. Its highest point exceeds 10,000 feet and is subject to change, since the mountain, named Agung, is an active volcano. It is quiet now, but back in 1962 Agung blew, killing a lot of people and ruining considerable real estate. A verdant island forested with palms and pines and laced with rice paddies, Bali impressed me as being largely unspoiled despite the crush of more than two million people. Their culture enhances nature. Pagodas stand comfortably on the terraced slopes; ornate carvings in wood and stone decorate shops and homes; Balinese women wrapped in patterned sarongs and bright sashes walk to market with parcels balanced on their heads; Balinese men wearing umbrella-sized straw hats toil morning and evening in the fields, taking refuge under thatched roofs from the midday sun. Over the next two weeks Maryrose and I motorbiked over much of the island seeing the sights and sometimes making spectacles of ourselves.

Monday, January 19, I was at the post office when it opened. There were a couple of letters but no money. Later in the day I tried to call Billy and got nowhere. Well, I did get through to Singapore, which was inadequate for my purposes. Tuesday I drew another blank at the post office. I fired off a cable. At the Bali Beach hotel I asked the manager, Mr. Hagen, if he would cash the check I was expecting. He said he would if it were for no more than $250. But he warned me not to be optimistic about getting money through the postal service, because the service was so bad that stamps were often stolen off the envelopes. That evening I wrote back-up letters to Billy and my sister Sallie and gave them to an American doctor who was flying out the next day. He said he would mail them in New York.

At the hotel I met Bob Young, an Australian who worked for Qantas Airlines. He and his wife, Philippa, had been in Bali about a year and, despite the communications problem, they loved the place. He touted me to the cremation that was taking place Wednesday in a village near Denpasar. You haven't seen Bali, he said, until you've seen a Bali cremation.

Next morning after breakfast at the Delicious restaurant and an unproductive stop at the post office, Maryrose and I set out to find the funeral. That was not difficult; we just followed the tourists. In the village hosting the ceremony a Balinese lad of about 15 took us in hand and explained in fair English what was going on. Festivities began at about 11 P.M. with a feast and, thanks to our new friend, we were soon munching on rice cakes, fried bananas, and other delicacies. After helping ourselves to seconds, we stood by the side of the road and watched the procession march to the temple, thence to the cremation grounds. The body lay atop a wooden structure about 20 feet tall, which was borne by a small army of pallbearers, followed by gaily dressed dancers and musicians. Carvings, colored streamers, and flowers festooned the pyre. That afternoon all this went up in flames. Although we didn't stay to see it, the fire was fed throughout the night, until the body was reduced to ashes. These were then thrown into the sea, and the charred bones buried. Our young guide told us that the richer the deceased was, the more elaborate the funeral—and the higher the pyre. I would judge that the person we saw cremated had been pretty well-off.

Thursday began with my usual call at the post office with the usual dispiriting results. It ended with Maryrose and I hopping on the Honda and heading for a monkey dance, which, I was told, depicted Balinese history. The dance was being performed at a temple about ten miles from Denpasar, and to get there, you had to go to a small village and turn right at the crossroads. In order to make such a turn on a motorbike, you have to lean inward as you twist the handlebars; the faster you go, the more you lean. We cruised up to the intersection at a brisk rate, and I leaned on the turn just like you're supposed to. But Maryrose, riding behind me, thought I was leaning too much; so she shifted her weight and leaned the other way. Unable to steer properly, I lost control halfway through the turn. What made it bad was that a truck was coming, and I was on the wrong side of the road. Instead of squeezing the brake lever, I panicked and hit the gas. The bike lurched across the road, missing the truck by a hair, jumped an irrigation ditch, and sped down a narrow path scattering ducks, pigs, and people. Mothers grabbed their children and rushed inside. Men shook their fists and yelled Balinese obscenities. Dogs barked. I wasn't about to stop and apologize. Dodging trees, I bounced across the irrigation ditch back onto the road and kept on going. After that, the monkey dance seemed a little dull.

On Friday morning I went to the immigration office to have our visas renewed, then to Rina's to negotiate another week's use of the bike. My credit was still good. After lunch at the Delicious, I rode out to the airport, where Bob Young introduced me to a meteorologist. He upset my plans for going to Christmas Island. We would be sailing smack into the northwest monsoon, which meant a lot of headwinds and rain. The alternative was to try to skirt the monsoon by going to the Cocos Islands, then on to Mauritius, almost 4,000 miles away. The length of the passage meant we would risk running short of food. While we had stocked up on plenty of canned goods in Australia, supplies diminished every day we stayed in Bali. And since I was now down to about $28, we would be dipping into the boat's stores even more. The question was: Should I continue to wait for a check or sail while there was still food enough to last a month? What I did that evening was blow part of the 28 bucks on food and drink at the hotel, winding up in the Youngs' room talking politics until 4 A.M. It was an international affair, including, besides the Youngs, Maryrose, and myself, a French couple and Bob and Barbara Schrappe, who were German. Bob was beverage and food manager for the hotel.

The following day I saw Bob Schrappe at the hotel and mentioned that I planned to take Bob Young sailing on his birthday tomorrow—Sunday. Would he and Barbara care to join us? "Let's have a birthday party," he suggested. "You supply *Molly Brown,* and I'll bring the food and wine and whiskey." I thought it was a splendid idea. About nine o'clock next morning the Schrappes arrived with the food packed on ice in Bali Beach hotel containers. "Compliments of the chef," Bob quipped. The champagne was also iced. Philippa came aboard soon after, and we put up the awning and motored out of the harbor around to the lagoon in front of the Bali Beach hotel, where Bob Young was to meet us. At noon the hotel's motor launch sped toward us pulling Bob on water skis. He made a dramatic landing beside the boat and climbed aboard. Then the party began. We uncorked champagne and tore into stuffed lobster while Maryrose cooked thick steaks. A few minutes later the launch returned, and guess who was in it? Mr. Hagen, the hotel manager. He waved as the launch came alongside. There really wasn't much we could do but invite the man aboard. Although Mr. Hagen hadn't known until now that the hotel was provisioning the party, he took it like a gentleman. He sat down and drank some of the hotel wine and ate some of the hotel lobsters and hotel steak and never said a word about the hotel containers lying on the deck. At least, he didn't say anything then. Later I suspect he and Bob Schrappe had a talk.

We sailed all afternoon, arriving back at the quay just before sundown. After our guests left, we motored into the harbor and dropped anchor. During the day we tied *Molly Brown* to the quay, but couldn't leave her there at night, for rats would jump on board. It's hard to sleep with rats pattering on deck.

I thought surely I would hear from Billy on Monday. At least on Tuesday. By Thursday I was so downcast, I said to hell with the post office. Maryrose, however, insisted that I check anyway; she had a feeling. Sure enough, there was a cable from Billy stating that $250 was on the way to the bank in Denpasar. If he had already wired the money, it would certainly take a couple of days to get here. Rather than hover around the post office, Maryrose and I decided to take a short holiday in the mountains. Bob Young suggested we bike up to the village of Kintamani, which sits on the rim of an old crater. From there, he said, you could look across a valley and see Mount Batur steaming, for this volcano is still active. Intrigued by the photographic possibilities, I bought a roll of color film for my Nikkormat and edged a bit closer to bankruptcy.

We left Denpasar after lunch. It took us three and a half hours to travel the 35 miles to Kintamani, which wasn't too bad when you consider we walked part of the way. The ride was a piece of cake the first 20 miles or so, with the Honda scooting smoothly past terraced fields. But after that, the grade became steeper with every succeeding mile. With its burden of about 300 pounds, the Honda couldn't quite make it. The bike lurched and jumped, then, the transmission gone, quit all together. Maryrose and I pushed it the last two miles up the mountain.

In the village we inquired about lodging for the night and were directed to a house down a pine-shaded path. The proprietor there told us every bed was taken, but that we could sleep on mats in front of the fireplace. The fire felt good, since it gets chilly up in the mountains at night, and I willingly forked over the two-dollar flop fee. Our fellow guests were hippies, seven or eight carefree souls from Australia and New Zealand, and one, I think, was French. They shared their wine and whiskey, we our cigarettes in the ski-lodgey room. After chatting awhile, we all strolled down to a family inn and had the blue-plate special—rice, tomatoes, and bacon. And beer, of course. Then it was back to the lodge and early to bed because I wanted to be up at daybreak to photograph the steaming volcano silhouetted against the sun.

At 5 A.M. I looked outside into a thick fog. I

could not see the Honda parked ten feet away, much less the volcano. We waited a couple of hours, had breakfast at the inn, and waited some more. The fog persisted. About ten o'clock Maryrose and I got on the Honda and started coasting down the mountain. That worked all right until the road leveled out, then we had to get off and push. In the tiny village of Bankli, I asked around for a handyman who repaired motorbikes, discovered there wasn't one, and kept on pushing. By now it was noon and we were halfway to Denpasar, too damned far to walk. I told Maryrose we would park the Honda, hitch a ride, and return later with Rina to fix the bike. In a few minutes the Kintamani-to-Denpasar bus came down the road, and I flagged it. I asked the driver if he had room for a broken bike. He opened the back door, and we pushed it into the aisle. We couldn't have strapped it on top of the bus, for there were coops of chickens there.

We arrived in Denpasar at 1 P.M. and rolled the crippled Honda to Rina's house. While we tinkered with the bike, a bad squall roared in, toppling trees and knocking down telephone poles. I was afraid to think what had happened to *Molly Brown.* Secured by only one anchor, she had probably been dashed against the rocks. After the storm blew out, Rina let me borrow the Vespa while he worked on the Honda. Maryrose and I raced through town and across the causeway, dodging debris and splashing mud all the way. What a relief to find *Molly Brown* in one piece. She had dragged a couple of hundred yards, but there was no damage, not even to her awning, which I had left up.

After re-anchoring the boat, I decided to take a swim. As I was coated with grime and sticky with sweat, I needed one. So did Maryrose. We put on our bathing suits and stepped into the Avon tied beside *Molly Brown.* Using the rubber boat as a jumping-off place, we splashed around like a couple of kids. Then one thing led to another, and it wasn't long before I had her bathing suit off. I pitched it into the Avon, my swim trunks following immediately. Now, if a boat had passed by and someone on it had looked in our direction, this is what he would have seen: two heads close together and an arm locked onto the Avon. That's all. If he had noticed that the heads were bobbing in unison, he might have concluded that he was witnessing the top part of an aquatic ballet. But if he had, he would have been most unimaginative.

After the ballet, I unlocked my arm from the rubber boat and released my partner, and she released me. We should have kept on dancing. For we had failed to notice that the current was going out—at about five knots, I would judge. It carried us with it, sweeping us inexorably, as they say, out of the harbor and into the ocean. It took a minute for this to dawn on me, and by then we were maybe 200 feet from the boat. My first thought was to swim across the current to a fishing village. But how would that look? Two adult foreigners wading ashore without a stitch of clothes on. On the other hand, swimming back to the boat demanded much of a spent man. Not as much, however, as standing naked before a stranger; therefore, I flung myself against the current and, yelling to Maryrose to follow, gallantly fought my way back to the dinghy. She beat me there by two lengths. Decent again and back on *Molly Brown,* Maryrose poured us a drink and said, "Ree-shard, what crazy theeng you theenk of next?"

She got her answer Sunday. I took her to a cock fight. I love cock fights. When I was a kid growing up in southern Maryland, we used to have cock fights out back of the barn. In rural Bali they have them every Sunday. With the Honda back in working order, Maryrose and I set out through the paddy fields after lunch. We found the place about 1:30, a good-sized wooden building banked with grandstands. It cost us two dollars to get into the noisy arena, and that almost broke me. Wagering was heavy, with fistfuls of rupiahs changing hands after each fight. Of necessity, I abstained, concentrating instead on the action. By southern Maryland standards, the fights were rather slow; the Balinese didn't pit their birds as rapidly as we do down home. After five or six duels, a short fellow came around collecting admissions in his outstretched straw hat. I thought we had paid for an entire afternoon of cock fighting, but evidently this was not so; you had to keep feeding the kitty to stay. Maryrose took exception to what she considered to be gouging, and began raising hell with the poor man. He couldn't understand a word she was saying, but her expressions and the shrillness of her voice needed no translation. She made ugly faces, hurled insults at the crowd, and swung her arms wildly. Before long we were encircled by angry, hissing, booing Balinese men. Though I did everything in my power to shut Maryrose up, short of belting her, she continued trying to incite a riot. I finally pulled her out of there, and none too soon. In another minute I believe those people would have mobbed us and thrown us into a rice paddy and let us rot for a thousand years. Overanxious to leave, I flooded the Honda, which delayed our start enough for Maryrose to start popping off again. That reinvigorated the spectators, and they came hooting and hollering. The Honda fired and we bolted down the road as the first stones fell.

I didn't say anything to Maryrose until we were back on the boat. Then I told her politely but firmly that if she ever pulled a trick like that again, she no longer would be welcome aboard *Molly Brown*. I hated to lean on her, but at the same time, as a guest in a foreign country I felt some obligation to keep my crew under control. Maryrose apologized and said she would never misbehave in port again. I had my doubts.

Monday morning I went to the bank to pick up my $250. It hadn't come in. I asked the teller to call the main branch in Djakarta to see if the money had been sent there. He agreed to do this and said he would have an answer by 2 P.M. When I returned, he told me no message had come through and to check with him again at nine the next morning. I did, and the news was bad. No money for me in Djakarta. I didn't know what to think. But I did know what to do. We had to leave. There was no other choice. Better to eat *Molly Brown*'s stores while crossing the Indian Ocean than while here in port. I hated the thought of landing in Cocos without money, without even the price of a drink or enough to buy a roll of film. A yachty! That was the level I had sunk to, a penniless yachty. At least until we made Mauritius.

I dropped by the hotel to say goodbye to the Youngs and Schrappes. Bob Young invited Maryrose and me to dinner, but we didn't go. I felt too badly. In the log I wrote, "The first day of my life I did not eat a piece of food." Next morning I breakfasted on a large bowl of split pea soup, which was filling enough. Now it was time to clear with customs and come clean with Rina, who was expecting to get paid for the use of his Honda. I rowed to the quay, where I met the captain of a small tanker that had come in during the night. I swallowed my pride and hit him up for some gas. All he had was aviation fuel, he said, but after hearing my sad tale, he lent me some money—$60 Singapore or $20 American. With that I bought gas and a few groceries. As for Rina, I gave him my personal check for $65, explaining that he would have to send it through his bank to the States before it could be cleared, which, considering my experience, might take awhile. I told him it was a hell of a way to have to do business, but it was the best I could offer. If for some reason the check didn't clear, I promised I would send him a money order when I got back home. As things subsequently turned out, the check cleared quickly; so I'm confident Rina received his money.

Rina rode me back to the quay, stopping on the way so I could notify the bank to return to the sender any money sent to me. I bought an old gasoline drum at the dock for two dollars and filled it with 50 gallons of fresh water, which is all Maryrose and I would have to drink for a month. There wasn't a drop of whiskey left on board. At 2 P.M. we motored out of the harbor. I had a smile on my face and exactly one dollar in my pocket.

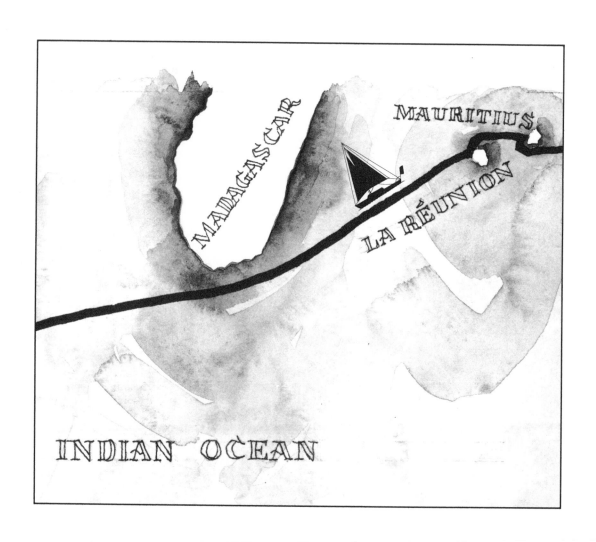

MADAGASCAR

MAURITIUS

LA RÉUNION

INDIAN OCEAN

Chapter 10

Thursday,
February 5:

Maryrose and I both have colds. She is running a temperature of 103°, which worries me. We get a fresh westerly at 1400, and I hoist the main and No. 1. Maryrose is too sick to eat dinner, but I'm encouraged that her fever is down one degree. The wind is on the nose at force three, and we are self-steering and beating with the main reefed.

Friday,
February 6:

Squall at 0300. Before I can come up on deck *Molly Brown* heads up into the wind and gets in irons, losing her headway. The mainsail luffs, straining the rigging to the breaking point. A gooseneck fitting snaps, and the boom swings loose, banging against the mast. I drop the mainsail. The boom crashes into the cockpit. I lash the mainsail around the boom and the boom to the deck and the cabin. That's all I can do until daybreak. I go below dripping water and fall into my bunk. At 0600 Maryrose fixes breakfast despite her cold and seasickness. I down a bowl of hot soup and get to work repairing the gooseneck with a pair of locking set screws and two-part epoxy, which takes 24 hours to set. Wind moderates at 1400, but the sea is still too choppy for motoring. I set the working jib;

however, we can't drive into the headwinds without a mainsail. There isn't a damned thing we can do except wait until the glue hardens.

Saturday, February 7: Rough seas at 0600. We're still floundering. Four hours later I hoist the main. The gooseneck holds. Maryrose's cold has improved, but mine is worse. I reef the main at 2000 and go to bed.

Sunday, February 8: After an early morning squall, the weather clears and a gentle westerly continues all day. My cold is better. I know it is because I can taste again. After dinner of rice-and-tuna casserole, I sit on the cabin and smoke.

Monday, February 9: Peaceful night with no squalls, and beautiful sunny morning. The wind freshens throughout the day, blowing at force five by dark. Hello, monsoon.

Tuesday, February 10: I am up all night, as monsoon winds continue to blow. The seas are building and *Molly Brown* is pounding. Maryrose is too seasick to fix dinner.

Wednesday, February 11: A nerve-racking night, with the screaming wind, dead on the nose, blowing force five and six. All morning it howls. I reef the main, but we're still carrying too much sail. I hank on the storm main to shorten canvas. High seas continue to batter us. At 1400 I change course, tacking south-southwest. I have to do something. Wind and seas remain high at midnight.

Thursday, February 12: We heave to at 0400, for the wind is gusting at force six. At 0700 I hoist the jib but can't make headway in the high seas. At noon I tack northward hoping for improving conditions. I shorten down to a storm jib and reefed storm mainsail—good balance but little driving power. The seas are too big to drive into them. Miserable sailing. Seas moderate some at 2300, and I sleep for first time in two nights.

Friday, February 13: Squalls rake us all morning. *Molly Brown* shudders, takes the pounding, and comes up for more. She can stand the abuse but her crew can't.

We've about had it. Maryrose can't hold her head up she's so seasick. It is pure torture to go on, but I'll be damned if I'll turn back. With the wind behind us, it would be comfortable, easy going. However, returning to Bali dead broke would be the worst possible mishmash we could get into. The thought of starting out again across the Indian Ocean is too painful. We'll go on. A pack of killer whales pay us a call at 1500. One of them swims under the boat and breaks the self-steerer blade latch wire. That's Friday the thirteenth for you. The wind moderates to force four in the late afternoon. Maybe our luck is changing.

Saturday, February 14:

After tacking southwest, I repair the self-steerer but decide to steer the boat myself. *Molly Brown* seems to go better with me at the tiller, especially in puffy air. Despite squalls before noon and after, the boat is moving well. Maryrose fixes rice, canned peas, and canned salmon for dinner. Food is becoming a problem; there may not be enough to last until we get to Mauritius. I go to bed a little after midnight but can't sleep.

Sunday, February 15:

Are we out of the monsoon? The seas are down considerably, and the wind is west-southwest at force three. Beautiful morning. I change course at 1300 and hoist No. 3 jib. Then, wouldn't you know it, the wind honks up and the ocean starts churning again. We can't seem to make any westing no matter what I do. It's never before been this bad for so long. Maryrose is seasick again, but there's not a damned thing I can do about it.

Monday, February 16:

Beautiful morning after excellent night's sleep. I take my coffee on the cabin top and watch boobies diving in a school of small tuna. Moderate breeze veers from west to southwest and back. I hoist the full main, charge the battery, keep busy making minor repairs.

That afternoon the wind came in hard again on

the nose, but it blew itself out during the night. I could sense things were going to get better. By dawn all the curls were down, and, for the first time in 12 days, there was a fair breeze out of the southeast. It was the nicest thing, I think, that's ever happened to me. I hoisted the main and hanked on No. 1 genoa, and *Molly Brown* charged ahead as of old. For the past several days I had been trying for more southing, figuring that maybe farther down I could pick up a favoring easterly tradewind. Now we had it instead of the northwest monsoon. No more pounding; no more drenching squalls; no more sleepless nights. At least not as many.

By tacking south, we kissed off any chance of making Christmas Island. A celestial fix the evening of February 17 positioned us past it and more than 150 miles below it. We aimed for Cocos, 500 miles west and slightly north. A mere pinprick on my chart, the atoll would be as easy to miss as an ant hole in a cow pasture; and I wanted to be spot on. With the sun directly overhead, I had no luck with noon fixes— frustrating but, as things turned out, not critical, for my star shots were successful. What was critical was our food and water situation. Water we could replenish in Cocos. However, we wouldn't have money to buy food until we reached Mauritius, 3000 miles away. On the nineteenth, I jotted down in the log: "Rice and canned ham for breakfast—nice for a change." We had long since run out of eggs and fresh supplies, living now almost entirely out of cans, and sparingly at that. We did have flying fish, of course, when the little rascals would cooperate and fling themselves aboard.

At 5 A.M. on Sunday, February 22, my alarm clock rang, routing me out of bed to shoot the stars. Two and a half hours later we made landfall dead ahead. A young Australian in a small boat motored out to meet us as we entered the harbor and told us where to anchor. He advised us in a friendly way that yachts weren't well received in Cocos. A dependency of Australia, the atoll has for generations been run by the Clunies-Ross family as a coconut plantation. Visiting yachtsmen used to enjoy hospitality at the plantation manor house, but inevitably they wore out their welcome. Almost apologetically, the young man—I think he was the plantation manager—suggested we might be more comfortable on neighboring West Island. There sprawled Cocos Aerodrome, once a refueling stop for commercial jets. For emergencies, a crew still maintains the airfield and weather station, though planes are few and far between.

I motored over to a long wooden quay built for tankers that called here, but now abandoned to shore birds and strays like *Molly Brown.* In the village, laid out along the lines of a military base, we met Ken Shaw, representative of the Australian government, who invited us to his home. Acting as customs and immigration official, he stamped our passports, then asked us if we would like to stay for dinner. While his wife Andrea and Maryrose chatted in the kitchen, Ken and I had a cold beer on the front porch. Believe me, that was a supremely satisfying moment. I cradled my glass in both hands lest I spill a drop.

Ken recalled how the Danish yacht *Sawankhaloke* had come into Cocos—the hard way, over the reef blocking the southern end of the atoll. Her crew, new at navigating, had driven her up there, tore her bottom out, and walked ashore. They stayed there six months, sponging off the islanders while scrounging for materials with which to repair the boat. Since Claus Keating, the captain, was a master shipwright, workmanship was no problem. In fact, Ken said, Claus had built the boat in the first place, and he had done a beautiful job. Probably the boat should have been in a museum rather than at sea, for neither Claus nor his brother Annis, pretending to serve as navigator, were sailors. The third male member of the crew was a German writer named Werner—first name or last, I don't know, for Ken didn't say. The cook, a pretty Danish girl, was called Daughter.

Next morning, while Maryrose ran our dirty clothes through Andrea's washer, I checked the weather station for low pressure systems between here and Mauritius. Hurricanes sweep across this time of year, and I didn't care to tangle with one. The weather report was perfect—no lows moving anywhere that might affect us. After I filled the water cans, we would leave. I wouldn't stay one more day on Cocos if I couldn't buy someone a beer. We said our thanks and goodbyes and motored to the "forbidden" part of the harbor, where there was a beautiful anchorage. But one thing spoiled it—a boat, a grubby 28-footer obviously owned by a yachty. We met him, a fellow named Carl. He was an American, a journalist, and flat broke. He bummed a toothbrush from me. Misery may love company, but I doubt it. I had enough problems without listening to Carl's, so I didn't waste much time with him. Maryrose and I had supper in the cockpit and went to bed early. At daybreak I motored out of the channel, then hoisted the main and No. 1 genoa. There was a fair breeze out of the southeast. We had 2400 miles to go, and I still had my dollar.

Wednesday, February 25: In the trades and moving well at five knots. A morning sun line shows we've made 160 miles the past 24 hours. Wind is steady out of the southeast at force four. In the afternoon I read *Georgian Century, 1714–1837,* by S.E. Ayling. When I don't have troubles, I read about someone else's.

Thursday, February 26: Cloudy at sunrise but clearing by 0700. *Molly Brown* is charging westward under reefed main. Breeze falls to force three in late afternoon. Having nothing to drink, I write letters. One to Connie begins with a weather report: "I am alive and doing well out in the middle of the Indian Ocean. The weather is beautiful, a light southeaster with clear skies."

Friday, February 27:
Arise 0600 and change sails (pole jibs) as wind has gone easterly—just what we need, as we have made enough southing for a few days. I get a good noon sight, the first in two weeks. Wish I could remember what I did right. In the afternoon I write more letters, including one promised to my neighbor's 13-year-old daughter, Cathy Hartman. I send her a weather report also but throw in a few storms to make it interesting.

Saturday, February 28:
Light squalls through the night, but clear at dawn. More trouble with the gooseneck, only this time it's the slide-track fitting. The aluminum screws are corroded, and I can't get them out to replace them. I'll work on it again tomorrow. Evening fix is 16°30′ south latitude, 87° north longitude—1750 miles out of Mauritius.

Sunday, March 1:
After breakfast of rice and canned peaches I worry about the gooseneck fitting. Finally lash it to the mast with a lot of line. It won't slide, but it won't fall off either.

Tuesday, March 3:
Breeze pipes up to force four and I pole out headsails. At dusk the wind increases to force five, and I drop No. 2 jib to lessen our northwesterly heading. We have logged more than a thousand miles in seven days. I am very satisfied with *Molly Brown.*

Wednesday, March 4:
Sunrise is breathtaking, bathing everything glowing pink. I have several exposures left in the Nikkormat and I spend one now. After coffee I play with the shortwave radio and pick up Johannesburg, which is comforting. In the afternoon I read *Blackcock's Feather.* Maryrose says it is a child's book. So it is. I charge the batteries, rewire the alternator, shoot the stars at 1900.

Thursday, March 5:	The barometer is falling. Yesterday morning it read 30.08 inches; this morning it's 30.02. I try for a weather forecast on shortwave but can't pick up Mauritius. The barometer falls to 29.99 at 1530, holds the rest of the day.
Friday, March 6:	I'm up at 0600 to find barometer down only .01 inch. Wind drops, and we're becalmed at midday. I read *2001: A Space Odyssey.* Maryrose is fishing, has yet to catch anything on this passage. We could use a little fresh meat to go with our rice and tinned rations. Star fix at 1900.
Saturday, March 7:	After poling out double headsails, I start the motor to recharge the batteries. At noon I take a sun shot, then recheck last night's star fix. I plotted it wrong, will shoot again tonight. No, I won't. Evening squalls see to that.
Sunday, March 8:	Lousy sailing all night and light, fluky air this morning with numerous squalls. At 0800 we're becalmed, and I start to motor. Engine runs hot. I shut it off at 1030 and pole out twin jibs. While becalmed in afternoon, I repair water pump, replacing impeller, and work on masthead and spreader lights. Star fix at 1900 tells me we have 730 miles to go—hungry miles, for we're running out of food. There is coffee for two days, rice for five or six, and enough canned food for a week if we stretch it.
Tuesday, March 10:	Good sailing yesterday; more of same today. We are 500 miles out at noon. We gamble with the unknown for dinner. Wrappers have come off several of the cans and we open one. Surprise! Beets. We open another mystery can. More beets. After dinner (main course, beets) I work on the engine. Batteries are dead.
Wednesday, March 11:	Leftover beets and warmed-over coffee for breakfast. I pick up "Voice of America" on radio but not Mauritius. Another hour's work on the engine pays off; I crank it up and charge the batteries. I skip

lunch—no more beets, thank you—and shoot a sun line. We're too far south. I pole out the genoa on the port side, and the aluminum pole breaks. We splurge for dinner—corned beef hash, rice, and saltines.

Thursday, March 12: I get up at 0500 and shoot four stars. We made only 80 miles yesterday. Barometer fell .04 inch during night but is now rising. I pick up Mauritius on the radio but can't get time ticks; according to radio station time, my Accutron is two minutes off. Good sailing all day under the main.

Friday, March 13: Bad squalls with lots of rain all morning. Can't pick up Mauritius, can't get a noon latitude, and the barometer is falling too fast for comfort. I might have guessed we were in for it; this is Friday the thirteenth again. I lash everything down. Barometer drops to 29.85 at 1530. We might get hit tonight. Rice and canned tomatoes for supper, and that just about does it. We have one can of mushroom soup, a few crackers, and a little rice left; that's enough if we aren't blown off course. We'll stand watch tonight.

Saturday, March 14: It's raining when I take the watch at 0100. Barometer is still falling. I alter course from southwest to west-southwest. Barometer levels off at daybreak; wind backs to northwest. We have sailed through a small low. Landfall at 0700. Serpent Island is dead ahead. We'll have to beat around it. Mauritius radio reports low pressure moving south. We're out of the woods.

We motored southwest until we sighted the undulating land mass of Mauritius. Port Louis, its capital and our destination, lay on the northwest side of the island, which presented a problem, since we made landfall farther south than expected. We could either motor northward and chance piling up on rocks in the dark or swing down and coast up the opposite side. The latter would take longer but, despite our empty cupboard, I thought it was safer. So that's what we did. Next morning we entered the harbor under power, detouring around two Russian ships and a Russian submarine. For a moment I wondered if World War III had been declared while we were at sea, for the sub looked like a battle casualty with its stern sticking out of the water. But since no bombs were falling and the Russian sailors aboard the two salvage ships waved at us, I figured the sub must have hit a rock or something and nosed over. Or maybe the captain had too much vodka, forgot he was in shallow water, and gave orders to dive. Whatever the cause, the sub was in an embarrassing position and, presumably, so was the captain.

Health and immigration officials came aboard quickly, found everything in good order, and welcomed us to Port Louis. Ordinarily I can't wait to get ashore after a long passage, but this being Sunday, I knew we couldn't do much to improve our situation. Nevertheless, we motored to a quay, tied up *Molly Brown,* and walked into town. By 10 A.M. we were strolling up the main street, almost deserted at this hour; everything was closed except bars and restaurants, which might as well have been for all the good they could do us. True, I still had my dollar, but was reluctant to spend it on something as trivial as, say, coffee and sweet rolls. When you're down to your last buck, you try to make it count. For instance, a crap game is a good place for a last dollar. But I didn't see any this morning in Port Louis; everybody was in church, I guessed. So I kept my dollar, and we walked until we found the building I was looking for—the Qantas Airways office. Before we left Bali, I asked Bob Young to forward my mail to Qantas rather than the post office. He said he would and also gave me the name of the district sales manager here—Frank Lamb. Like everything else, the place was closed, but at least I knew where it was. Maryrose and I walked back to the boat, took an afternoon nap, then had a light supper—rice without any trimmings. That was all right. Tomorrow we would dine like kings.

Qantas opened at nine the next morning, and I was there with minutes to spare. When I got in, I asked for Frank Lamb. He checked the mail and brought out an envelope. I ripped it open, and out fell a letter from my sister Sallie, which was nice, but there was no money. What the hell had gone wrong? I couldn't put it together. "Frank," I said, "I've got to call my brother Billy. Can you help me?" He suggested the American Embassy. Thirty minutes later I was explaining my problem to a sympathetic receptionist. I told her I did not have enough money to make a phone call, send a cable, or buy a postage stamp. She said not to worry, picked up the phone, and within minutes Billy Zantzinger was on the other end of the line.

He asked how I was, and I said fine; how are you doing? He said he had no complaints. I asked if he had seen Kyle and Richard lately? Yes, he replied, they were fine and missed me. He also remarked that my financial situation was not absolutely desperate, although I was getting a lot of mail from Internal Revenue. He couldn't straighten out the tax mess because my accountant had left Washington unexpectedly and taken the books. "With no way of finding your accountant," he said, "and you in Mauritius, wherever in hell that is, I don't see that you have much to worry about." This certainly made sense to me. "By the way," he continued, "have you received the money I sent to Barclays bank?" I was just on my way over there, I told him. I said goodbye to Billy, thanked the receptionist, and walked the two blocks to the bank.

It was an active place crowded with Europeans, Indians, and Chinese. The tellers wore crisp safari suits, the female employees mini-skirted uniforms—a lovely sight to a man who had been at sea for almost 40 days. But money was what I had come for. I walked to the window marked foreign correspondence and told the clerk my name. He looked at my passport and asked what denomination traveler's checks I wanted. I could have kissed him. With $2,000 in my pocket, I felt like I had robbed the place. Maryrose was scrubbing the galley when I returned to *Molly Brown.* Put away the Ajax, I told her, and I'll take you to lunch.

Besides being an old town, Port Louis was not the cleanest one I ever saw, but it did possess a certain charm that appealed to me. Strictly maritime, it bent around the harbor like a horseshoe—a pretty sight at night when strands of lights reflected off the water. Here mingled bearded sailors, barefoot blacks, Chinese merchants, English businessmen—some carrying umbrellas. Indian ladies moved quietly in flowing saris; ebony-skinned Mauritian ladies balanced baskets on kerchief-covered heads; tanned French ladies clicked along on spiked heels. Bicycles darted among Peugeots and Austins. Exotic odors from quaint shops, each with an awning thrust over the sidewalk, wafted through open doors to tempt the passersby. Maryrose and I were tempted. We stopped in a confectionary for double-dip ice cream cones. We sipped iced soft drinks through straws at another place. In a curbside market we bought a bag of fresh fruit. From one store to another we went like a couple of kids blowing their allowance, sampling this and that, always washing it down with something cold and wet. It didn't make any difference what it was—Coke, fruit juice, even water—so long as there was plenty of ice in the glass. We had a wonderful lunch—a real movable feast. The last place we visited before returning to the boat was Ling Fat's, the A&P of Port Louis. Its long rows of shelves were stocked with tinned foods from all over the world. I asked a Chinese boy who was sweeping the floor why the inventory was so large and varied. "We ship chandler for many many ship," he replied. He also said they delivered right to the boat. We bought a few items—all we could carry—and said we'd be back later with a complete shopping list.

That afternoon I moved *Molly Brown* over to a water barge and topped her tanks. It was there we met two gentlemen in business suits who had been admiring my boat. The short fellow was Roger Hardy, the tall one Jacques—I never did get his last name as it was French, and it is all I can do to get English names. Having had the foresight to buy a bag of ice and a bottle of Scotch, I invited them aboard for cocktails. Both had lived on the island all their lives, and both spoke French. Roger, a happy-go-lucky bachelor about my age, also spoke English. Owner of a masthead sloop built of wood, he was curious to see *Molly Brown*'s fiberglass construction. He marveled at how well she was equipped for a 35-foot boat, being particularly impressed with the shower and hot and cold running water. These I always showed to visitors, though I rarely told them the water heater never worked and we could not carry enough water to shower at sea. I liked for people to think that *Molly Brown* had all the comforts of a luxury liner. Roger owned an automobile dealership, and when he learned that I'd had trouble with the gooseneck fitting, he said he would send a mechanic down to fix it the next day. That evening he, Maryrose, and I had dinner at a nice hotel near Plaisance airport. As Roger drove over a narrow, winding road past sugar plantations, he gave us a lesson in Mauritian history. For one thing, I learned that Mauritius was the home of the dodo bird. A delightful chap, Roger didn't stop talking until he began working on a mouthful of rare steak.

"Fried eggs, bacon, toast. Wow!" That's what is

written in the log for the following morning. Breakfast was served by Maryrose at nine o'clock in the cockpit under the awning. The sun was shining, and the trades were blowing gently. We were at the Molly Brown Hilton. During breakfast a harbor launch came alongside with our mail and the daily weather report— a welcome service provided by the local port authority. Later, not one but two mechanics from Roger's garage showed up. He had explained that business was slack, and had been since the island, once a British crown colony, gained independence in 1968. Now Europeans were leaving for greener pastures. Roger was all for independence, but he hated losing his customers. The mechanics worked all day and wanted to work that evening, but I sent them home at five; it was, after all, cocktail time. Unexpected guests, a Swiss couple from the only other foreign yacht in the harbor, motored over in their dinghy and had a drink with us. They asked how long we intended to stay, and I said no longer than a week. Theirs was the standard yachty answer: "You can't see anything in a week." I thought—but didn't say—that if they got their asses off the sailboat and looked around a little, they could see a hell of a lot in a week. That evening we had dinner with them at the Merchant Navy club and watched television from bar stools. The program was "Gunsmoke" with a French soundtrack.

The mechanics were back next day, and we repaired everything on *Molly Brown* that needed fixing, including a stuck valve and a cracked alternator bracket. Maryrose had gone shopping at Ling Fat's. When she returned with a truckload of groceries, I asked: "Where in the hell are you going to put all that stuff?" "You worry about ze boat; I worry about ze food," she replied. Pretty damned cocky for a cook, but I really couldn't complain. Besides, she said she spent only $150. That evening Roger came down, and we had a party. I proceeded to get drunk and jumped overboard. Why, I don't know; I suppose to sober up.

The next day began on a pleasant note. Roger sent a car and driver down to take us on a tour of the island. Our first stop was a large sugar mill, where we met Claude Lejeste. He looked more like a white game hunter than a wealthy sugar mill operator. After a short lesson in the growing and refining of sugar, we were introduced to Noel Maurel, who designed boats. He had built yachts for both Roger and Claude, and now he was building one for himself to enter in the Cape Town to Rio Race. The event, scheduled for the following January, meant nothing to me at the time. I had not the slightest notion I would be racing *Molly Brown* against 60 yachts from a dozen countries. That's the way it worked out, however; and *Molly* didn't do badly. Finished nineteenth.

After lunching with Roger and Claude at a Port Louis hotel, Maryrose went shopping and I returned to the boat, where I still had chores to perform. One was taking on gas. I motored over to the gas dock, removed the bung from the inspection hole, shined a flashlight in, and saw that the tank was nearly dry. I then went up on deck, removed the cap from the fill pipe, stuck in the hose from the gas pump, and began filling the tank. From this position I could not see the meter on the tank, but that didn't concern me, for when the tank is nearly full, the air vent makes a whistling sound, signaling me to shut off the flow. Keeping my ears open for that whistling sound, I began pumping gas. After about half an hour and no whistle, I grew suspicious and went below to see where all the gasoline was going. It was, I discovered, going into the whole damned boat. Gasoline filled the bilge and stood two inches above the cabin sole. One spark and *Molly Brown* would go off like a hydrogen bomb. I could see tomorrow's headlines: "Americans Blow Mauritius off Globe." With the aid of a friendly policeman, I cleared everybody from the dock, pumped the gas out of the bilge into the harbor, and washed down the boat inside and out. There must have been 50 or 60 gallons of gas in the boat, and for a minute I was puzzled as to how it got there. Then I saw the bung. I had forgotten to replace it when inspecting the tank.

It took me a good hour to clean up the mess. The job completed, I sat down on the quay and lit a Lucky. About that time Maryrose walked up and asked what I was doing. "Smoking a cigarette," I said. "What does it look like I'm doing?"

Since the boat still reeked of gasoline fumes, I took her out to dinner. That was a mistake. For when we returned, *Molly Brown* was in a shambles, with drawers pulled out, bunks torn apart, lockers broken into. I grabbed the flashlight I kept under the cockpit seat and beamed it at the hatch. It had been pried open; that's how the thief got in. The first thing I checked for was the sextant. It had not been touched. Both radios were in place. What the hell were they after? I looked for my cameras. Both were gone. So were $1600 in traveler's checks, my Accutron wristwatch, Maryrose's clothes—not that she had a lot, but now she had none. She was crying. We climbed into the Avon and rowed to the quay to report the crime to the harbor police. Gilbert and Sullivan couldn't have improved on what happened next. And Sherlock Holmes would have seethed with envy.

The duty sergeant called the chief inspector. The chief inspector rushed to the station, sized up the situation, posted a guard on *Molly Brown,* and drove us to his home. "At my house we can have a drink, and you can tell me the whole story," he said. It was now 1 A.M. Two hours later we were still telling our story, drinking the chief's booze, and listening to him discussing the American space program. A well-educated Indian, he knew far more about moon shots than I did. After assuring us that his men would retrieve every item stolen from *Molly Brown* within 48 hours, he invited us to dinner the following evening. Then he drove us back to the quay. We graciously declined his offer of a police car and driver for the remainder of our stay in Mauritius, explaining that Roger had already taken care of our transportation needs. I didn't think we needed two cars.

Maryrose was making breakfast when a police launch came alongside. Two husky Indians swung up over the life line and introduced themselves as detectives assigned to the *Molly Brown* case. Then they went right to work searching for clues, dusting for fingerprints, and in general making a bigger mess than the burglar had. I asked one of the detectives how he hoped to recover the items. He shrugged and said, "We have ways." After lunch Roger drove me to the bank, where I reported the checks stolen. I was told I could pick up new ones tomorrow. On the way back we stopped at the police station. The two detectives were making progress. They had recovered the Accutron, which was good news, since it served as my chronometer.

That evening Maryrose and I were whisked in a police car to the inspector's flat, a neat but unpretentious place overlooking a racetrack. He was immaculate in his tropical uniform, his wife graceful in white lace. Their three teen-age children—a daughter and two sons—were politely inquisitive; they wanted to know all about America and the places we had been; they were trying to reach out and make some small contact with a world they had heard about but could never hope to see. The thought made me sad. I wished I could have taken them with me. After a delightful home-cooked meal of curry, pickled eggs, and other exotic dishes, we had coffee and brandy; then it was time to go. The inspector summoned a police car to drive us back to the quay. Not once during the entire evening was the *Molly Brown* case mentioned.

Around noon the next day, Maryrose and I were having a sandwich in the cockpit when the police launch pulled alongside. One of our detective friends stepped aboard and came right to the point. Did we have the numbers of the missing traveler's checks? I told him that I did not, but I would gladly go to the bank (which I intended to do anyway), get the numbers, and bring them to his office. Very good, he said; we have a suspect.

The Central Investigation Department was housed in a frame building fronted with a railed porch. When I arrived, the detective was sitting in a chair on the porch, his feet propped against the rail. His sleeves were rolled up, his tie hung loose, his pistol dangled from his belt. He arose, flashed a big grin, draped a large, dark arm around my shoulder, and ushered me into a back room. In the center stood a round table with a light hanging directly overhead. At the table sat three detectives busily filling out various forms. They took no notice of us. In the far corner of the room a frightened Indian boy of about 16 sat in a chair, his arms handcuffed behind him. The detective nodded toward him and told me that the watch and traveler's checks were found in his mattress. What about the cameras and Maryrose's clothes? The kid won't talk, the detective said. What are you going to do with him? I asked. The detective inquired when we were leaving. It was now Thursday, so I thought we would stay over the weekend and sail Sunday night about 11 o'clock. "Good," the detective said loudly.

"At 11 o'clock Sunday we will be on the quay with a large burlap bag. Inside the bag will be the kid. We will tie the bag to the stern rail of the boat. When you pass the inlet out where the sharks feed, cut it loose." I said okay and walked out.

The threat of being fed to the sharks had the desired effect. The kid confessed, Maryrose got her clothes back, and I was reunited with my cameras. But one of them, my Nikkormat, had been all but ruined by salt water when the thief swam ashore with the loot. My underwater camera was unharmed, of course. I left the damaged camera with a watchmaker who, Roger swore, could fix anything, although it sometimes took awhile. If it wasn't ready before I left, Roger promised that he would ship it to Cape Town. And that's eventually what happened, even though I stayed in Mauritius several days longer than scheduled. The reason was hurricane Louise. Our daily printed weather forecasts tracked her westward movement across the Indian Ocean, and for awhile she was taking dead aim on Mauritius. Not until she turned southward did I consider it wise to go to sea.

There were a number of vessels in Port Louis waiting for the hurricane to make up its mind. One of them was the magnificent 300-foot frigate *Libertad.* Training ship for the Argentine navy, she was on a goodwill voyage around the world. Roger and I had seen her come in under full sail, her steel sides as white as foam, her gilt figurehead glinting in the sun. A hundred men high in her rigging looked like birds roosting; but as she floated into the harbor they scrambled about furling her great snowy sails of Dacron. I've never witnessed a more breathtaking sight. Yes, I went aboard her; nothing could have kept me off. And the evening before she and *Molly Brown* sailed, I was aboard her again, with Maryrose, as invited guests for a seated dinner. What an array of gleaming crystal and silver and polished wood. Had the meal been hot dogs and lemonade instead of rare Argentine beef and hearty red wine, I would not have minded in the slightest, so grand was the spectacle.

The morning after was just as spectacular as the night before—at least to me. Others might have seen it as ludicrous. As *Libertad* was nudged by a pair of tugs toward the channel, *Molly Brown* under power swung along beside her. Several launches trailed us, Roger in one, the chief inspector and his aides in another, all waving goodbye and wishing us *bon voyage.* And Claude Lejeste was there, circling in his plane. Now the *Libertad* crew swarmed aloft and set her cloud of sail. At the same time I ran up the main on *Molly Brown* and broke out the big genoa. Two vessels under sail, both circumnavigating, cleared the harbor together, then headed in opposite directions—the three-masted frigate for Australia, the little sloop for South Africa.

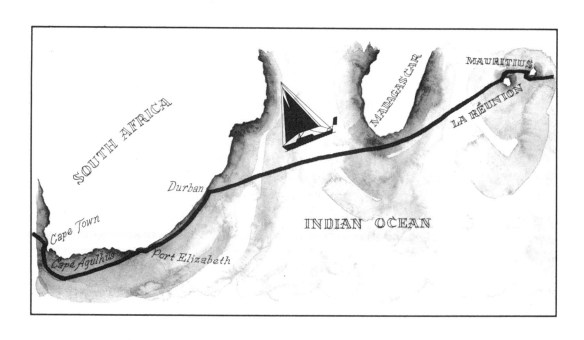

Chapter 11

It was great to be back at sea. I love the islands and the people you meet, but I like to keep on the move. Durban, South Africa, lay 1600 miles southwest, and according to the pilot charts, it shaped up as a nice passage. We shouldn't run into rough weather until we neared the continent. The first five days out I would have to pick up some southing to get under the tip of Madagascar, then it would be westing all the way to Durban.

In the afternoon I dropped the big genoa and hanked on the No. 3, as the breeze had been freshening all day. By supper time the sea was rough, Maryrose was sick, and I was hungry. I warmed a can of vegetable soup and washed it down with half a bottle of claret, which, as everyone knows, is good for the stomach. Before going to bed I rolled the main down to the third batten, and woke up at two in the morning to drop it all the way. Dawn found me on the foredeck removing No. 3 and hanking on the storm jib. At 0730 I sighted the island of La Réunion off the port bow.

Before leaving Mauritius, I had alerted Radio

Port Louis that I would be calling in this morning for a weather check. The operator heard my signal, responding with a hearty, "Good morning, *Molly Brown*." His next transmission shook me: "I have some bad news for you. Louise has changed course and is headed straight for Mauritius. She is due to hit here tonight and should be on top of you sometime tomorrow. You should consider going into Reunion." I thought he was absolutely right.

Now I knew why hurricanes have feminine names. Though they follow a predictable pattern most of the time, they occasionally can be drastically unpredictable—just like a woman. As we motored into the walled harbor of Porte des Galets, Maryrose handed me a cucumber sandwich. How unpredictable can you get? Roger Hardy had been in this harbor many times. He told me it was better protected than Port Louis, and a small boat could weather any storm in it. The industrial section of the harbor, which contained the heavy equipment for loading bulk sugar, was bulwarked with a stone retaining wall taller than *Molly Brown*'s mast. At the dock near the wall was a small fishing ship, and I asked her captain if I could tie alongside her. He said be my guest; just make her secure. In a few minutes we were snugged in. It was blowing a near gale now, but in the harbor there was hardly a ripple.

I had just finished securing *Molly Brown* when our first caller arrived. Dressed in white, he came down the ramp and headed directly for the fishing ship, which led me to to conclude that he was a doctor hurrying to treat a sick sailor. I was wrong on both counts, as I discovered when he stepped from the ship's rope ladder to the deck of *Molly Brown*. He introduced himself as André Bacquet, a dentist, not a physician, and the owner of the only fiberglass boat on the island—a 28-foot sloop. He had seen *Molly*

Brown sail into the harbor and wanted to examine her, not a patient. Fiberglass fanciers are that way; I'm that way myself. Well, I showed André the shower and the other frills that didn't work, then we sat down and talked sailing and drank Scotch. André was basically a single-handed sailor. "My wife will not get on a sailboat," he said in a French accent barely understandable. So every year he would sail alone to the Seychelle Islands, about 900 miles north of here, stay a couple of weeks, then return to his practice refreshed. I felt sorry for the man. Imagine having a wife that would not go sailing with you. He insisted that I have a look at his yacht berthed on the other side of the harbor. I didn't much relish getting out in the wind, which was really screaming now, but he had been so nice I couldn't refuse. We climbed up the ramp to the top of the wall, and it was all we could do to keep from being blown off. Finally we made our way to his boat. She was a real mess below; I doubt if André had ever cleaned her. It was easy to believe his wife had never been aboard.

I rolled out of my bunk early the next morning and tried to call Port Louis, but the damned ship-to-shore radio wouldn't transmit. It didn't matter; I picked up a Port Louis weather report on shortwave. Louise was still bearing down on Mauritius, although she had slowed some. I thought of poor *Libertad.* She was probably in the middle of it about now. André and his son Philip (the second officer on the fishing ship) showed up after breakfast and volunteered to take me and Maryrose on a tour of the island. I asked if it wasn't a bit windy to be sightseeing. André said there was nothing to worry about—they have blows like this all the time—so we piled into his car and off we went, stopping first at his home to pick up his wife and daughter. André had told me that Madame Bacquet (Maria was her first name) served as the island's midwife; she had delivered more than 2,000 babies in 20 years. As we turned into his driveway, I figured it would be a toss-up between her and Hurricane Louise.

I couldn't have been more mistaken. We walked into the combination home-clinic-dental lab, and Maria stepped out of the delivery room to greet us. What a strikingly handsome woman. Her eyes were dark and intense, her hair coal black, her skin deeply tanned. She might not have spent any time on her husband's boat, but she was obviously no stranger to the beach. Her full breasts strained at her white uniform blouse, and from the looks of her shapely legs I assumed she made house calls on foot. André introduced us, and she smiled and said something to me in French. It was a shame that we could not converse, for I'm sure we would have found much to talk about. As it was, we still tried to communicate during the ride over Reunion's rumpled green countryside. I could not imagine how any man in his right mind could leave a woman this lovely for a miserable trip to the Seychelles. André, perhaps reading my mind, told me that they always took separate vacations. In fact, day after tomorrow he was flying to Tokyo, weather permitting. With the way the wind was whipping and the clouds were scudding in, I thought his chances for a delay were excellent. I knew damn well *Molly Brown* wasn't budging until the trees stopped bending over trying to touch their toes.

We had a pleasant lunch in St. Pierre, a small village at the southern end of the island, and André insisted on picking up the tab. I could have used a friend like him on Cocos, when I was down to a dollar. We drove back across the eastern, or windward, side of the island. From the heights we could look straight down into deep gorges and, near the coast, hear the sea thunder against the cliffs. It would have been a hell of a drive on a dark, windy night. With those gale winds rocking the car, it was pretty hairy even at midday. André dropped Maria off at the house, and we went down to *Molly Brown* for a drink. I picked up Port Louis weather on the radio and heard that a class II warning had been issued for Mauritius.

The next day, Sunday, Louise clobbered Mauritius and, according to radio reports, was responsible for considerable flooding and wind damage. She was due to hit us at midnight. I walked around *Molly Brown*'s decks checking lines and fenders. With the aid of two crewmen from the fishing ship, I strung a hundred feet of three-quarter-inch line from *Molly Brown*'s bow to the quay and another line from her stern to the retaining wall. By late afternoon the harbor was becoming crowded with small boats seeking refuge from the storm. At 10 P.M. my barometer registered 29.75 and was falling fast. The wind was blowing a gale. Rain pelting the cabin top sounded like a cow pissing on a flat rock. I climbed into my bunk to await my first hurricane, and damned if I didn't fall asleep.

When I awoke at daylight, the wind had moderated and the rain had slacked off to a deluge. I paid a call to Philip next door, who had just received the latest weather bulletin. Louise was 60 miles offshore and curving south. By 9 A.M. the sun was trying to break through. Philip invited Maryrose and me to accompany him to the airport. It was only about 15 miles away, but it took us an hour to get there, for the road had been washed out in places. André and Maria were already there. After we saw André off, Maria asked if I would drive her back to Porte des Galets, since the road was so bad. Maryrose, I should explain, was doing the translating at this time; then when she decided to ride back with Philip, Maria and I were on our own. Despite the language barrier, we somehow managed to communicate. I understood, for instance, when she indicated a desire to see *Molly Brown*. But I didn't understand why; this woman supposedly hated boats. I parked the car and helped Maria down the ramp and across the deck of the fishing ship, though I really don't think she needed any help; her grip was stronger than mine. While I was trying to devise a graceful way of getting her onto my boat, she took matters in her own hands, jumping from the deck of the fishing ship to the cabin top of *Molly Brown.* She was like a cat. I must have looked astonished, for she burst out laughing. When Maryrose, arriving with Philip soon after, hopped aboard in similar fashion, I never batted an eye. Philip, though, seemed surprised she was so light on her feet. He should have seen his mother a few minutes earlier.

The sound of sizzling bacon awakened me next morning. Maryrose had breakfast going early. "We have been on Reunion long enough," she said. "Let's sail." I walked down to the jetty to see if we could get out. Even though Louise was no longer a threat, the seas were still rough. As a matter of fact, five ships were steaming outside the harbor waiting for a chance to come in. I thought it best we stay in port today. Maryrose said I was chicken.

Wednesday, April 1:

The barometer is 30.10, the sky is clear. We motor out of the harbor at 1100 and immediately bang into high seas. The wind is out of the south at 25 knots and forward on the beam. Maryrose wisecracks about me being in such a damned big hurry to leave. I feel like spanking her, but I would never strike a seasick woman. We take a pounding all day, then a squall comes through at 2300, and the wind backs to the southeast. A fair breeze.

Thursday, April 2:

Maryrose is frying tomatoes southern Maryland style, the way I taught her. Storm petrels are dancing on the crest of waves and in the troughs—a good omen. For one thing, it means fish are about; and Maryrose, like John Tucker, wants her share. Before breakfast she puts two lines out, one with a spoon, the other with a rubber squid Philip gave her. While I'm taking a noon sun shot, she hooks a small tuna, which we have for lunch. Perfect sailing all afternoon and evening, a little cool at night.

Friday, April 3: Another beautiful morning. Our southeast breeze is holding steady at force four. After charting our position at noon, I open a little book I bought in Mauritius called *Teach Yourself French.* After an hour of teaching myself French, I try a few words on Maryrose, and that breaks her up. I know the French are a sex-oriented people, but why did they have to confuse their language with all that feminine and masculine junk? Now, everybody knows that a sailboat is a she—I certainly never heard of one referred to as a he—yet the French word for sailboat is classed as masculine. I put aside the book, for it is all Greek to me, and pick up my copy of *The Adventures of Captain Cook.* How the Captain could work a ship like *Endeavor* through all that coral without a chart is a mystery to me. Well, it is good to be out in the ocean without any coral to worry about.

Saturday, April 4: I'm up at 0630 after a good night's sleep. This is the first time since leaving the States that I have gone 36 hours without having to touch a sheet or adjust the self-steerer. I spend the afternoon sitting on the coach roof and watching the sea, as I often do. Over the port bow I notice two columns of water on the horizon. They disappear, then in a few minutes I see them again, this time much closer. We had seen whales before, but none as big as these. The nearer they came, the larger they got. "Deek, zay are going to seenk us!" Maryrose exclaims. I do not think so, but I know the choice is entirely the whales'. Swimming along together, they pass by apparently oblivious to our presence, like lovers strolling through the park. I watch them till they are out of sight, then go up to the forward cabin to take a nap. Maryrose is stretched out in the main cabin. I am curled up under my old army blanket dreaming impossible dreams when a blast from the loudest ship's horn I have ever heard rattles my eardrums. My first thought is that some son of a bitch is about to run us down in broad daylight. I kick off the blanket and fly up on deck with blood in my eye. There the big bastard sat, a super tanker with her engines throttled back and her officers on the bridge looking at us through glasses. They wave, and some joker comes down on that horn again. Maryrose stands there in her underwear and shrieks obscenities. I tell her to go below and get some clothes on before the tanker decides to send over a boarding party. A big cloud of smoke pours out of her stack, and the ship steams off. I am a charitable man, and after some thought, I have come up with a plausible explanation for the ship's odd behavior: One of the officers must have picked us up on the horizon with his glasses and, not seeing any movement on deck, surmised that *Molly Brown* was a derelict. Reluctant to steam away from a boat in distress, the captain had the ship bear down on us, then went for the horn. Maryrose doesn't buy that, and I'm not sure that I do; but I can't think of any other reason why a tanker would go out of its way to scare the hell out of a couple of people on a little yacht. I sight Madagascar off the starboard bow at sunset. It's quite a sight—hulking black mountains slowly blotting out the huge red ball. The wind backs to the east at 2200, and I drop the main.

Sunday, April 5:   After a restless night watching for ships, I get up late and scramble a couple of eggs. No sense in bothering Maryrose, busy with her fishing lines. I

166

adjust the shrouds after trimming the mainsail, then pole out No. 2 jib on the main boom. An hour of peace and quiet ends with Maryrose screaming, "Help!" I dash up to see what's the matter. She's hooked a big pointy-nosed shark and is trying to reel it in without much success. I wrap the heavy fishing line around the geared genoa winch and start cranking. "Get the shotgun," I yell. If we can get this monster aboard I'll blow its brains out and take his picture. Maryrose brings up the shotgun and finds me holding a piece of limp line. It's just as well I lost him; the shotgun wasn't loaded. I nap until dinner, then stay awake until daybreak, for we are in the shipping lanes.

Monday, April 6: Sunny morning, cloudy afternoon, with wind increasing to force five. Good sailing.

Tuesday, April 7: I pole out No. 2 genny after breakfast, then bait a line with a flying fish. A nice dolphin takes it as soon as it hits the water. I haul the fish in and clean it for dinner. With everything going so well, I decide to turn on the pressure water system. Now Maryrose won't have to use the hand pump under the bridge deck. The wind drops in the evening to force two. I take the midnight watch.

Wednesday, April 8: At 0200 a ship looms astern of us, but we're not in her way. The wind dies at 0600, and I start the engine. By noon we have a breeze out of the southwest, which continues to back and freshen during the afternoon. Rough seas all night.

Thursday, April 9: After breakfast we sight our first albatross. What a bird! Gliding over the stern of the boat, it looks like a 707 approaching Kennedy Airport. It circles once and flies off—in good health, I swear. I did not take a shot at it, though it was within easy range. But shortly after it departs, the wind drops and the sails are flopping. By noon we are becalmed on a glassy sea or, as Coleridge put it, "As idle as a painted ship upon a painted ocean." We sit there the rest of the day and most of the night, but there's one consolation: Unlike the Ancient Mariner, we have plenty to drink.

Friday, April 10: We're nine days out and have 195 miles to go. If the wind comes in on the nose, it won't hurt now. Brave words, those; I have them for dinner since I can't get anything else down. At twilight the wind hauls to the northeast and blows hard all night. I say to hell with beating into it and heave to.

Saturday, April 11: Force seven winds at daybreak with lots of whitecaps. They remain high until 1000, then peter out. We're becalmed in a rough sea. I motor for 30 minutes and find a breeze. It comes in strong from the southwest, and I hoist No. 4 jib. At 1800 the wind moderates and backs to the west, and we get a shower. The wind freshens again, this time out of the northwest. It's been all over the compass.

Sunday, April 12: I'm up at 0200 after five hours of much needed sleep. We are in the shipping lanes near the coast, for there are ships all around, and we can see many lights ashore. Darkest Africa is lit up like a Christmas tree. I shoot the stars at first light and plot our position 35 miles north-northeast of Durban. After draining the water that has collected in the carburetor, I crank the engine and motor in.

It was a super Sunday—warm, cloudless, and calm. Surfers and sailboats were out in force, and I counted an even dozen ships lying at anchor outside the inlet. We anchored in the quarantine grounds and were soon boarded by port authorities and quickly cleared. They said we could tie up at the Point Yacht Club quay. An hour later we were in the yacht club lounge sipping gin and tonics. These people never heard of bourbon. A bearded fellow about my age walked up and demanded the check. "I am Bob Frasier," he said. "You should not have to buy drinks after a long passage." The news travels fast. Bob was ex-commodore of the yacht club, a first generation South African of British stock, and a bachelor. That last item interested me, for I was feeling much the part of a father anxious to see his only daughter wed. That evening Bob took us on a tour of the city and afterwards joined us aboard *Molly Brown* for a brandy.

I spent the next couple of days strapping down *Molly Brown*'s swing-and-sway gas tank, taking long showers, and quenching my thirst at the yacht club. It was there that Maryrose and I met the crew of *Sawankhaloke,* the custom-crafted schooner that hit the rocks on Cocos. Claus and Annis invited us to a farewell party they were throwing on the boat before sailing to Cape Town. It was a beautiful boat and a swinging party, which lasted all night. I didn't last all night, mainly because I'm a gulper instead of a sipper, but I stayed sober long enough to appreciate the romantic effect of kerosene cabin lights flickering against the rich grain of oiled teak. I also remember meeting Aussie yachties Allen Quigley and Thomas Bone ("call me T-Bone") and a good-looking blonde named Gail Temple. She was 22, British, and teaching art in Durban. After a couple of drinks, I asked her if she would care to take a quick peak at the famous *Molly Brown*. She said no, it took all the nerve she could muster to step aboard *Sawankhaloke.*

Gail

I awoke at 11 next morning with a thumping headache. Breakfast didn't help, so I took a nap. When I awoke, Maryrose was sitting in the cockpit chatting with a handsome young Frenchman who had immigrated to South Africa. We had dinner at his apartment—with brandy before and after—then immigrated to the Smuggler, a Durban night spot. While Maryrose and her friend were dancing, I noticed an attractive young lady at the table next to ours who appeared to be unescorted. I got up to ask her to dance and fell on my face. Brandy affects me that way.

Regaining my seat, which presently became a ringside seat, I resumed my role as spectator. As best as I can remember, the fight started this way:

Maryrose and friend were dancing when a young Canadian sailor, properly turned out in his blues, attempted to cut in. The Frenchman refused. Next dance the same thing happened. Undaunted, the sailor tried a third time, and Maryrose cut him down with a blast of French profanity. The sailor slapped her. The Frenchman belted the sailor, laying him out with one punch. I heard the blow; it sounded like a mule kicking a barn door. After that, everybody got in the act. Bottles broke, chairs flew, men cussed, women screamed. I never moved until I heard the sirens. Do your thing, legs, I prayed, and they did, carrying me through the kitchen and out the back door.

The following afternoon I was standing at the yacht club bar enjoying a cold beer when T-Bone charged through the door. "I've been looking all over this bloody yacht club for you," he said.

"Yeah, Bones, but I've been laying a little low today. What's up?"

Bones: "The girls want us to come for dinner."

Me: "What girls?"

Bones: "Gail and Mary."

I thought this just might be the change I needed. Mary, a British girl, was Bone's friend and Gail's roommate. In Australia Bones had been a truck driver, a kangaroo hunter, and a chicken thief. I never did find out what he did for a living in South Africa. Gail picked us up in her Volkswagen bug at 6:30 and drove us across town to her apartment. It was a nice flat on the top floor, with a balcony overlooking the Indian Ocean. The girls shish-kebobed lamb and I tossed the salad while Bones kept our glasses filled. After dinner he and Mary went to a dance. I volunteered to stay and help Gail with the dishes. One thing led to another, and next thing I knew, I was helping her do the breakfast dishes too.

Ordinarily, a trip to the zoo is not my idea of a swinging weekend; but, with Bones calling the shots, that's where we were going—to Zululand. Armed with a couple of six-packs and my camera, we sped northward along the coast to Umfolozi game preserve, where the wildebeests and warthogs play. At the Sundown hotel six porters struggled with our three small bags and had our tubs drawn before we got to our rooms. Business, as you might guess, was slow. But not the service. We spent the afternoon in the bush taking pictures, generally photographing the south end of animals going north, and returned for drinks and dinner. The food wasn't all that great, but Bones stowed it away like a starving elephant. Next morning he ate six eggs, which awed the waiters and alarmed the management, since meals were included in the lodging tariff. Bones left five cents South African as tip, and we drove up to Hluhluwe to see the famous white rhinos, which are gray. After I exposed several more rolls of film, we returned to Durban.

Anticipating the departure of Maryrose and dreading the prospect of cooking my own meals all the way across the Atlantic, I asked Gail that evening at dinner if she would like to sail to the States with me. She said she would have to think about it. I told her I was not looking for any great romance; but I believe, in my chauvinistic way, that a woman takes a statement like that as a challenge. Next day at lunch in the yacht club, she said she would like a little test run—to see if she and *Molly Brown* were compatible. The following evening, after she finished work, we motored out of the harbor; and I hoisted the main in a gentleman's breeze. Red lights were flashing when we left the harbor and again when we entered it; but I didn't pay them any more attention than I did to the guy in a launch who yelled to us on the way out. He was probably somebody I had met at the yacht club, so I gave him a wave and kept going. We had a nice little sail, returning to the harbor about 10 P.M. As soon as we entered, a harbor police launch came alongside, its loudspeaker commanding me to stop. Annoyed at being mistaken for a gunrunner or some other shady sort, I shut off the engine and made ready to protest my innocence. Or—and the thought staggered me—was it Gail they were after? Gail the diamond smuggler! That had to be it. Except for some back taxes, I was clean. Surely the IRS wouldn't come all the way to Durban, South Africa, to collect those crummy taxes, would they? It's not constitutional, is it? The officer stepped aboard, told me I had violated the law, and proceeded to write out two tickets—one for leaving the harbor without permission, the other for leaving and entering the channel against the red lights. Total: 150 rand, or about $200 American. At nine o'clock next morning I was sitting across from a very proper British port captain and apologizing for my ignorance of the rules. He laughed and pitched the tickets into a trash can. What are your plans? he asked. I said we were taking the first fair breeze to Cape Town. He said this wasn't the best time of year to go around Cape Agulhas in a small boat, but they would keep an eye on me. I thanked him and walked over to the yacht club, where I met Gail for lunch.

"I want to go," she said.

"Are you sure?"

"No, but I want to go." She would meet me in Cape Town in a couple of weeks, as soon as she got her affairs in order. Her main problem was to find someone to take over her duties at school.

The prospect of having a new crew for the trip across the Atlantic stimulated me. But why stop at just having one new crew member? Perhaps my daughter, Kyle, would be permitted to join us. And little Cathy Hartman. I had just received a letter from her saying how much she yearned to be an ocean-going sailor. That night I wrote to Billy, asking him to see if he could arrange for the two to fly to Cape Town. It was a long shot, but my luck was running pretty good. The only thing that disturbed me was Maryrose. She had shown no inclination of getting off in Durban, though I had hinted that this might be a good place for her to find a job. I sensed that she might want to go all the way with me to the States; but with her passport problems, that would create complications I didn't care to get involved in. She would have to get off in Cape Town whether she liked it or not. If she decided to fly home from there, I would ante up the air fare to Switzerland.

On Thursday, April 23, I called the meteorological office and got a good weather report. A low off Agulhas was moving out and a northeaster was moving in. I told Maryrose we would leave in the morning. Maybe we would catch up with *Sawankhaloke* in Cape Town.

Friday, April 24:

Bones makes the supreme sacrifice—gets up before noon to see us off. On the way to the channel, I call the port captain and request permission to leave. His reply: "Wait for the green lights; then you may go. Good luck and a fair breeze all the way." We motor past the breakwater and take a hard right. Pushed by a four-knot current and under power, *Molly Brown* is really rolling—up to ten knots. Valve sticks at 1630, and I get out the hammer. An hour later we're back in business. A breeze freshens out of the southwest at midnight. What happened to that northeaster the weatherman promised?

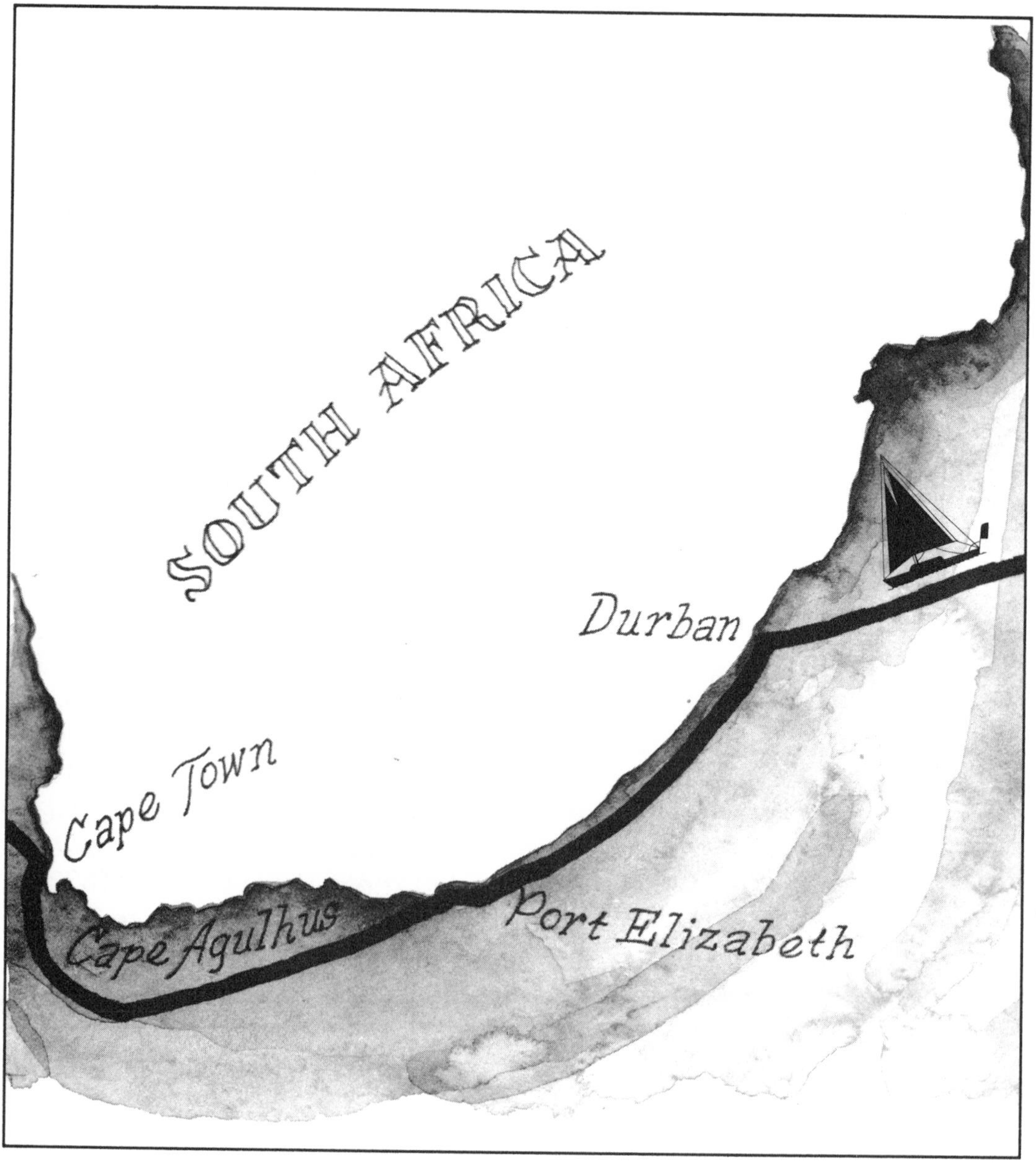
SOUTH AFRICA
Durban
Cape Town
Cape Agulhus
Port Elizabeth

Chapter 12

Saturday,
April 25:

It's blowing like a bitch and right on the nose. At 0100, in a cold, driving rain, I roll the main down to the third batten and hank on the working jib. At daybreak the wind honks up to force six. Nasty going all day. Maryrose is seasick, and I'm worn out from tacking back and forth across the shipping lanes. We meet a freighter about every 15 minutes.

Sunday,
April 26:

It is 0200 and I am sitting in the cockpit trying to stay awake. All I can see is black and water. All I can feel is rain pelting me in the face. All I can hear is a throbbing sound growing louder by the second. In a minute a mountain of cold, hard steel is towering over us, and I freeze as the ship shaves our stern. The son of a bitch misses us, but not by much. She was so close, I might as well have been standing in her engine room. At daybreak Maryrose stands watch while I grab a couple of hours' sleep. Sky clears at noon, and we reach down the coast as wind and seas moderate. In the evening the wind jumps all around the compass, but the current keeps us moving. We are now below the 32nd parallel, abeam of East London at 1800, Great Fish Point at 2300.

I decide to put in at Port Elizabeth to top our tanks and check the weather at Agulhas. After standing the midnight watch, I give Maryrose a compass heading across Algoa Bay, then go below and crawl under my army blanket. At daybreak we pass Bird Island and work into the bay. It's supposed to be stormy as hell, but I've never seen a more beautiful day. As we near Port Elizabeth harbor at 1600, I get on the ship-to-shore and request premission to enter. "Hello, *Molly Brown*, we have been expecting you," comes the reply. "Radio Durban told us you might pop in. Come through the breakwater, and you will find room to tie up at the fishing-boat dock. I'll send the customs chaps down."

Within an hour, *Molly Brown* was gassed up and ready to go. Then the weather turned bad, and we were socked in for the night. Next morning after breakfast I called the signal tower for a local weather report. It ruled out the possibility of a westerly, which was good news, since this meant we wouldn't be sailing into the teeth of the wind. Ten minutes later a gust out of the west damned near blew me off the dock. Well, if I couldn't sail, I would take a stroll. Leaning into the wind, I walked out to the end of the jetty and got drenched by flying spray. Turning back, I hiked into town, which could have been a slice of Detroit. From the stack at the General Motors assembly plant, wind-blown smoke rolled over rooftops like black fog. Giant wheels of steam engines squealed and spun on greasy track as they shunted heavily laden coal cars. Huge cranes ringing the harbor dipped their cable tongues into holds of ships, extracting morsels of machinery and bite-sized boxes by the ton. Longshoremen, their eyes smarting from coal dust, muscled loads into waiting lorries. This was not my Africa. I walked back to the boat.

The port captain, his whites a dazzling contrast

to the dirty town, was sitting in the cabin talking to Maryrose. I poured us a drink, and we chatted awhile. Could he be of any assistance? I said no—unless he could produce a nice easterly. That he couldn't do, though there were men in the bush, he remarked, who probably had a ritual for such a request. He would, however, alert a research ship working between here and Agulhas to come to our aid should we call. I thanked him and hoped it wouldn't be necessary. I also thanked him for taking the time to call on us. After he left, Maryrose asked me why, in this busy port, a small yacht like *Molly Brown* rated such a courtesy. I don't know, I said; do you suppose it had anything to do with the American flag flying off her stern?

That evening Maryrose and I had dinner in a small restaurant. Afterwards we stopped at a bar, where we met two Johannesburg businessmen—one of them in the construction business, the other in real estate. They drove us back to the boat in a new Mercedes, and I invited them aboard for a drink. Maryrose, perhaps awed by the new car, perhaps just making idle conversation, hinted that she might stay in South Africa if she could find work. One of the men assured her he could get her a job in Johannesburg. For a second I thought I had lost a cook and solved a problem. No such luck. Maryrose declined the offer. After they left, she told me she didn't like the guy's looks. I slapped her on the ass and told her to hit the sack. We're leaving in the morning.

Wednesday, April 29:

The wind is light out of the east. I radio the port captain and tell him goodbye. By 1000 we are out of the harbor and moving easy under the main and No. 2 genny. With a fair breeze, it's "wing and wing" all afternoon. I don't know how long the weather will hold, but it's lovely.

Thursday, April 30:

I take the watch at 0200. The wind has gone light, so I drop the main, the No. 2, and crank the engine. A stationary white light gleams on the horizon, 30 degrees off our starboard bow. There is no land there, and the light is not that of a ship. The phantom light grows brighter as we move past it. It is spooky to see something where there should be nothing. At dawn the light fades, and in its place looms an offshore oil rig. I motor right up beside it and pound on the cabin top, then I stick my head out of the cockpit and give a war whoop. This puzzles Maryrose. I explain that I'm getting even. We have good sailing all morning in a force six easterly. RDF line and star fix at 1800 shows we are 240 miles out of Cape Town. It turns cold after dinner.

Friday, May 1: Another delightful day. Though my pilot chart shows that chances for getting hit by a gale here is two out of three, we can't complain. I tell Maryrose we will be in Cape Town for dinner tomorrow. At dark I go on deck to see if the loom from Cape Agulhas light is visible. It isn't, for a squall is bearing down. I check the barometer, and the drop is unbelievable. A peek out of the main hatch tells me that the squall line is a vicious front. When we get to Cape Town, we'll have a sea story to tell. I put on my foul weather gear and safety harness and go up on the deck. While taking the genoa pole down, a blast of wind bounces me against the mast, taking the hide off the back of one hand. I reef the main as far as I can and hank on the storm jib. Now it's beginning to blow pretty good out of the northwest, and *Molly Brown* is taking a pounding. We are making damned little headway. By midnight it's not worth fighting, and we heave to.

Saturday, May 2: With the wind on the nose, we slug it out for a few hours and get nowhere. At 1000 the wind increases to near gale force. I drop the storm jib and lash the helm and let *Molly Brown* just lie into it. We're a lousy 110 miles out of port and hove to for the duration.

**Sunday,
May 3:**

At 0300 the wind moderates slightly. Maryrose makes soup for breakfast, but can't eat it. Too sick. I finish my soup, and here comes the wind again, blowing harder than ever. The self-steerer vane, vibrating in the wind, almost shakes the pulpit to pieces; I dismantle it. I remove the mainsail and lash on a storm main trisail—with five feet on the luff and about the same on the foot, it's a fine steadying sail for heaving to. At 1000 we are in a blowing gale and rugged seas. The storm is pushing us south—away from land and out of the shipping lanes. That's all right; we won't fight it. It continues to blow all day. The seas are large and violent, the meanest I have ever seen. There is no letup. At 2200 the gale is full strength, battering us with 50- to 60-knot winds. The howling is maddening. *Molly Brown*, buoyant as a cork, takes everything that's thrown at her and comes up for more. Confident she will ride out the storm, I have some more soup and go to bed.

**Monday,
May 4:**

Wind is down to force five; skies are clearing. After breakfast I reset the self-steerer vane and repair linkage to the blade damaged during the storm. With reefed storm main and working jib, we gradually work into the waves, beating but with little pounding. The cabin reeks of gasoline fumes; I open the hatches. Bilges are pumped out. At 1500 down comes the storm sail; the main, shaking out the reef, goes up. The barometer rises. The wind drops. *Molly Brown* races for Cape Town.

Ducking inside the shipping lanes, we reached up the coast until we sighted Cape of Good Hope light. Dawn, gentle and cloudless, saw us off Cape Point. With the wind behind us, the main and genny rapidly filled, boosting *Molly Brown* northward to Table Bay. Then Maryrose and I set to work—her cleaning, me stowing sails. Spic and span, we motored into the harbor with flags flying—the

American ensign, South African courtesy, and Sailing Club of the Chesapeake burgee. No one could have guessed that *Molly Brown* had spent the last three nights hove to off Cape Agulhas.

A launch from the Royal Cape Town Yacht Club came out to direct us to a slip—right beside *Sawankhaloke,* her huge red and white Danish flag floating in the light breeze. Claus sprang over to help me with the lines. "Where have you been?" he demanded. "I looked for you a week ago." I said, "Claus, we stopped at Agulhas three days to look for pieces of your boat." That evening in the Cattleman, a Cape Town steak house, the two crews swapped yarns over platters of rare beef and bottles of red wine. It was the first full meal for Maryrose in four days.

Early next morning I walked the two miles into town and picked up seven letters at the post office—one from Billy, six from Gail. She was flying in tomorrow for the weekend. When I returned to the boat, Maryrose was in full command. The immigration and customs officer had come aboard with the usual forms, which she filled out, declaring herself an outbound crew member. Maryrose handed me the forms to sign. Without a word to her, I asked the immigration officer if I might accompany him to his office. While driving in, I laid my cards on the table. I told him I had only one boat but two cooks, now that Maryrose was balking at leaving. He said I had a right to put her off, though I would first have to guarantee her air fare home, which I had already agreed to do. All his office needed was a letter from me and the ticket, and they would put her on the plane—bodily, if necessary. If they attempted to manhandle Maryrose, I thought, they had better double the size of their army. I filled out a new set of papers, thanked the officer, and hurried back for the showdown with Maryrose.

"I am your responsibility, and I am not getting off," she declared.

"The hell you are, and the hell you're not," I retorted.

She hadn't given up, and I certainly hadn't given in, when we arrived at the yacht club that evening for its German beer fest. But after a few beers and a chat with Claus, everything was settled amicably. *Sawankhaloke* was leaving Sunday for Recife, Brazil. Claus could use an extra cook, particularly one with a dowry in the form of $300 for air fare. Maryrose, if she couldn't go to the States, preferred South America over Europe. And she liked the idea of sailing with the Danes. It was all settled. Next norning she moved her belongings to *Sawankhaloke*. I wished her luck, and she said it had been fun.

The next time I saw her was 9 A.M., Sunday, May 10. She was on deck with the rest of the crew as the yacht club launch towed the engineless *Sawankhaloke* out of her slip and into the harbor. Maryrose appeared to be quite at home in her new situation. I waved, she waved; and once again we were strangers.

The void *Sawankhaloke* left was filled within a few hours by *La Salle*. Hal had been around Agulhas too—way out around. A storm had pushed him a hundred miles south, into the iceberg zone. For awhile, he said, huge waves crashing on the coach roof threatened to cave it in. But he and Sally and the kids toughed it out; and now, like us, they were on the way home. They would leave in a week. I would have liked for *Molly Brown* to sail with them, but that was impossible. Gail was committed at the school until the end of the month, which meant I couldn't leave before then. Besides, I was banking on some young passengers joining me about then. Meanwhile, I had few chores to attend to, not the least of which was restoring *Molly Brown*'s bright work. Eleven months of salt water had literally taken the hide off her; there wasn't a speck of varnish left. So, after putting Gail on a plane, I got to work sanding and scraping. In the evening you could usually find me at the stag bar of the Royal Cape Town Yacht Club.

It was there I first heard the following story from Henry the bartender, who swore that every word of it was true. The trouble began, he related, when the captain and crew of a small yacht dropped in one evening for a few beers. This being a stag bar, it was permissible to serve the male crew but not the captain, who, in Henry's words, was a horse of a woman in her late twenties. He politely informed her that she would have to do her drinking in the lounge. Her reply, Henry recalled, was right to the point: "I am the captain of that goddam boat out there, and if my crew can stand at this bar, so can I." Now, it so happened, that most of the men at the bar that night were ocean sailors, and none could find fault with her argument. The Amazon captain got her beer at the bar, and the cause of women's lib was served. But, as so often happens when you relax the rules, someone gets his head knocked off—in this case, that of the South African gentleman standing next to her. The captain, after having put a few under her belt—or girdle—allowed that, like any other good seafaring body, her's developed desires not easily satisfied. She then ripped off her clothes, stretched out on the floor, and informed the South African gentleman that he was first. When he declined the invitation, she accused him of lacking in manhood. The gentleman replied that he might not be a man, but there was no question that she wasn't a lady. Not about to take his insult lying down, madam captain sprang to her feet, grabbed a bar stool, and cold-cocked the South

African gentleman. Henry said the poor chap was hospitalized for two weeks.

I had dinner with the Autenreiths several times, and once I babysat for them, taking the kids to see *Patton.* We had a great time, which got me to thinking again about how much fun it would be to have youngsters aboard for the trip home. I called Billy and told him if Boots wouldn't let Kyle come, send Willie, his eight-year-old son. The suggestion left Billy with a slight attack of lockjaw. When he finally recovered his voice, he blurted that he would let me know in a few days. I assured him the worst part of the voyage was over, that it was all down hill from here on in. Besides, I argued, it would be a good experience for Willie—put a little grit in his craw.

While waiting for Billy to make up his mind and Gail to finish up at school, I kept busy on *Molly Brown.* After a hard day's work with the sandpaper, there would be dinner with friends and, afterwards, drinks on the boat—not very exciting but pleasant. One couple I got to know, Dolf and Nell Tiddleybrandy (I'm spelling it the way I heard it), joined me on such an occasion. And, come to think of it, there *was* a bit of excitement. Dolf, a husky, easygoing Dutchman, and I were sitting in the cockpit enjoying cocktails while Nell looked around below. It was a delightful evening, complete with full moon and balmy breezes. From our perch we had a good view of cars parked along the quay, the yacht club in the background with lights ablaze, and beyond that the lights of the city—in short, a very civilized scene. As we gazed upon it, Dolf called my attention to one of the cars. "Look," he said, "the fool has left his brake off." Damned if he hadn't. We watched the car roll down an incline, bump over the bulkhead, and splash into the harbor not 20 feet from *Molly Brown.* Dolf shook his head and laughed. "That," he said, "was my car."

La Salle sailed at 5 P.M., Sunday, May 17. Watching her go made me a little sad, for it was comforting to have her around, to talk with somebody from home.

Billy called on the nineteenth. Cathy Hartman and Willie were flying to Johannesburg Friday. That was wonderful news. I went over to the yacht club bar and spread the word about my new crew. In the States I would have been judged crazy for attempting to sail a little boat 9,000 miles with a couple of kids aboard. But these South Africans were used to hard-nosed sailing, and gave hearty approval to my scheme. In fact, Dolf said he would have been willing to let his young son come along if I hadn't gotten a crew. Thursday evening he drove me to the airport to catch a flight to Johannesburg. Dolf's car, by the way, ran fine. Except for the faded upholstery, you never would have guessed it had been in the drink.

The 707 was late and I was early; still I missed seeing the kids disembark. Finally I spotted Willie in customs, but not Cathy. I shouted a big hello and asked where Cathy was. Willie pointed to lovely young lady beside him. What a difference a year makes. She was a scrawny 12-year-old climbing trees the last time I saw her. Well, I couldn't send her home now. In the hour we had to kill before boarding a plane to Durban, where Gail would meet her fellow crewmen, Willie brought me up to date on all the news back home. When I asked him about Kyle and Richard, he said, "Uncle Dickie, they are as bad as ever." That was encouraging. Cathy, almost 14 and going on 18, set young men's necks to swiveling as we walked through the terminal. She liked the idea of being looked upon as a young lady rather than a kid, but thought a matronly lady on the flight from the States carried things too far. "My," Cathy mimicked, "what an adorable son you have." Willie snorted.

Willie

Cathy

Gail was waiting for us when we stepped off the plane. She and Willie hit it off right away. Cathy, I think, surprised her, for she gave her a long, searching look as if trying to fit my tomboyish description to the ripening form before her. Well, there was no way. Cathy had grown up. We followed Gail to her car and found we couldn't get in. She had locked the keys inside. Fortunately, Cathy had some of her clothes on hangers, one of which I reshaped into a hook and wedged through a slight opening at the top of a window. A few minutes of jiggling with the jimmy sprung the inside door latch, and we were on our way to Gail's flat.

We arrived to find the punch bowl brimming and good things happening in the kitchen. Mary, Bones, and Gail's colleagues had arranged a surprise going-away party. With visions of lions and tigers dancing in his brain, Willie hardly expected to find himself at a party. But he manfully swallowed his disappointment and downed two helpings of curried lamb. Then, mollified by my promise that we would see the rhinos tomorrow, he crawled into a bed and slept for 12 hours. Despite fatiguing plane rides across an ocean and a continent, Cathy managed not only to stay awake but to radiate substantial southern Maryland charm. By midnight she had one of Gail's art students moonstruck. At one point I thought he was going to walk off the balcony and crash and burn 22 stories below.

Next morning we packed sandwiches, loaded cameras, and headed for Zululand. Willie, full of vinegar and eager for adventure, alerted us with happy yelps to every springbok, baboon, and giraffe in sight. When we stopped, he was out of the car like a shot and into the bush, pausing only to click his Instamatic before tearing off in search of more game. Willie didn't capture much on film, for the instant he

185

arrived, the animals, and I mean all of them, departed.

We had dinner at the Sundown hotel, where Gail had made reservations. The waiters, remembering my face, weren't too anxious to serve us, apparently because of the loss incurred by the hotel the last time I brought a group here. But Bones wasn't along this trip, and we left them smiling with a fat rand tip. The next day was Sunday—white rhino day in Willie's book. We saw quite a few of them. From a respectable distance, of course. They weren't about to get very close to Willie.

On Monday, Willie and I flew to Cape Town, the girls to follow on Wednesday, after shopping for the proper seagoing togs. I reminded them that anything fancier than T-shirts and dungarees would be an extravagance. While Willie and I slapped on varnish, a mechanic tinkered with the engine until it ran like a new one. Except for provisioning and a fair breeze, *Molly Brown* was ready to go by the time Gail and Cathy came aboard. Gail and I spent all day Thursday shopping, me trying to convince her that we did not have the storage capacity of a freighter, she smiling sweetly and going right ahead ordering what she damned well pleased. One thing was for sure: We weren't going to starve at sea. Friday evening Cathy was called upon to babysit while Gail and I went out with Dolf and Nell. After drinks and dinner at the Cattleman and brandy at the yacht club, I was experiencing no discernible pain. Returning to *Molly Brown,* I fell off the narrow log raft that served as a quay. In the morning Willie wrote a letter to his parents, marking the envelope "confidential." I never questioned him as to its contents, but eventually I found out. "Tonight Uncle Dickie and Gail went out to dinner," he wrote. "Uncle Dickie got drunk and fell overboard." The next time I saw his mother, she said: "That letter sure did a lot to put my mind at ease."

Saturday I had the boat hauled and her bottom painted. Next morning she was back in the water taking on fuel at the gas dock. With stuff lashed to the deck and crammed into every niche, *Molly Brown* sat so low I thought she would sink. The trick was to keep her afloat until we reached St. Helena. By then we should have used up enough supplies to be sitting pretty again. At 2 P.M. everybody from the yacht club was down to see us off. With bells ringing, horns blowing, people cheering, I felt like Christopher Columbus setting out to discover the New World as we eased away from the dock and into the harbor. Fifteen minutes later the cheering had stopped and we were back where we started. I had forgotten to take on fresh water.

We motored all day and night through heavy shipping. With that traffic to contend with and a green crew to break in, I didn't care to beat into headwinds blowing out of the northwest. We would stay under power until we picked up the southeast trades. After dinner all hands donned jackets to ward off the chill air and gathered in the cockpit for school, as requested by the captain. You don't give ships much thought during the day, I told the crew, but at night you must be able to read their lights. For an example, I picked out a ship heading our way, pointing out that its masthead light, white and high, is the first to come into view. Next appears the bow light, also white. Lining up these two lights enables you to estimate the course the ship is steaming. Got it, crew? Aye, sir. To continue then: As the ship draws nearer, the red and green running lights become visible, providing positive reference as to which side the two vessels shall pass. Any questions?

We counted about 40 ships that night. It was a perfect classroom to teach international rules of the road.

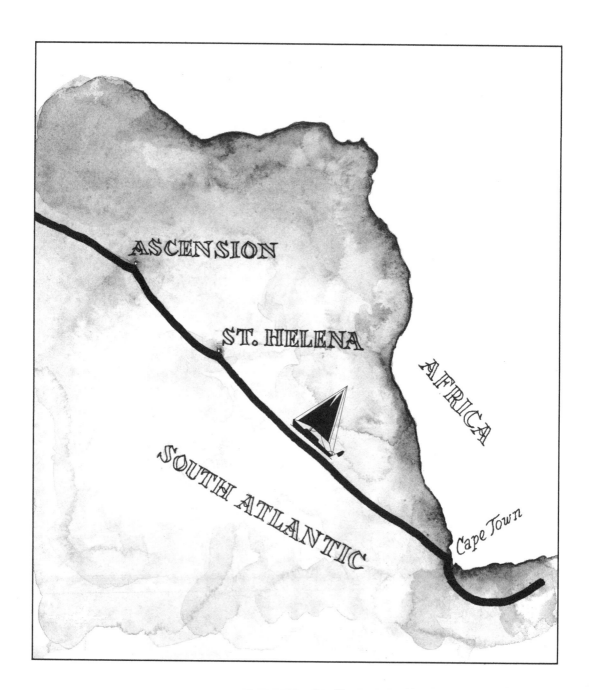

Chapter 13

**Monday,
June 1:**

We get a fair breeze at 0800, and up goes the main. It's so cold I can see my breath. I still can't get used to the idea it's winter down here. Breeze freshens to force five, and I pole out the working jib. Plastic gasoline drum lashed to the cabin top springs a leak. I roll it over the side. Sorry about that, ecologists. Good sailing all day and spaghetti for supper. Gail takes the first watch.

**Tuesday,
June 2:**

I relieve Cathy at 0300 and drop the jib, as it's not pulling. The wind is light, the weather warm, the barometer falling. I spend the afternoon working on the running lights. We are becalmed at 1800, and I crank the engine. Willie, complaining of a headache, doesn't stay up to watch me shoot the stars.

**Wednesday,
June 3:**

The wind freshens out of the northwest after midnight, later backing to the west. At 0400 I hoist the main. We're beating but with little pounding. I prepare breakfast: fried tomatoes, grits, scrambled eggs, marmalade. Willie has found his sea legs and appetite; he eats like a truck driver. Breeze drops to force one in the afternoon—not the best for making miles, but we're getting a little northing. Another day or two, and we should be in the trades.

Thursday, June 4: Wind is fluky, mostly out of the northwest, and we are making little headway. By nightfall the sea is flat. I crank up, and we motor all night.

Friday, June 5: We motor till 0800, then sit. Fuel is almost gone. At noon we're still flopping on a glassy sea. Gail and kids don swimsuits and jump overboard. I toss out the horseshoe life ring. Cathy finds a friend, a small gold and black fish that follows her around like Mary's little lamb. As she floats in the horseshoe, it nibbles at her toes. At 1400 a wind from the southwest—a fair breeze. Swimmers climb aboard, I shake out the main, and we are underway once more. The little fish is following us.

Saturday, June 6: Fluky winds, poor sailing until 1600, when our southwester returns. It continues to freshen, blowing force five by midnight.

Sunday, June 7: We're moving nicely, but the self-steerer isn't working well with the main. Rather than shorten sail, I do the steering. The waves build and crest behind us, a wall of water advancing on the stern of the boat. We catch a little spray as *Molly Brown* drives off the top of the waves. Passengers feel a bit queasy and lie low. I have a cold, some fever. Gail prescribes penicillin. Nobody stands watch tonight. We seem to be out of the shipping lanes.

Monday, June 8: Wind backs to the southeast during the night. We're finally in the trades. I pole out the headsails as we are now downwind. Crew perks up, and we have a gin game before dinner. No watches again tonight.

Tuesday, June 9: Light air, clear skies, and it's getting warmer. Kids take a swim at noon, and I take pictures. Gail spends afternoon sunning on deck. Another card game, then hot dogs for dinner.

Wednesday, June 10: No breeze in the morning under cloudy skies. Girls make oatmeal cookies in the afternoon, and I clean out the tool drawer. After dinner I raise No. 2 jib as wind is freshening out of the west. It backs to the southeast, driving *Molly Brown* at six knots.

Thursday, June 11: I'm up at 0700 to hoist No. 3 jib as breeze continues to freshen. By noon it's blowing force six, and *Molly Brown* is charging. Gail, feeling good, serves up baked ham, lyonnaise potatoes, spinach with mushrooms for dinner. Sure as hell beats hot dogs.

Friday, June 12: Breeze has moderated, but we're getting along. Rain in the afternoon. Kids are starting to grumble about being cooped up. Willie is seasick. I tell them it's all part of ocean walloping.

Saturday, June 13: Willie is cranky, Cathy isn't speaking to anybody, and Gail is making gingersnaps. Clouds leave after lunch, improving dispositions. Evening star fix puts us 320 miles out of St. Helena. Willie says he's going to eat all the ice cream on the island. Gail plans to spend four days in the tub. Cathy still isn't talking.

Sunday, June 14: This morning I give Gail her first lesson in celestial navigation while Willie fixes breakfast. Hot dogs. Cathy, breaking her silence, announces she will prepare dinner. Sun line puts us 270 miles out. Wing and wing trade-wind sailing in the afternoon. After dinner—macaroni and cheese—Gail and I sit on deck, look at the moon, have a drink. The British don't mind drinking without ice, and I don't mind drinking without ice either if I don't have it.

Monday, June 15: Good sailing, but kids are unhappy. They have had lines out every day and still have yet to catch a fish. I get a good fix at 1800. We have a hundred miles to go.

At five o'clock the next morning I shook Gail and asked her to make breakfast early. Then I woke Willie and told him to get Cathy up, a procedure Willie loved and Cathy hated. By 0630 I could see St. Helena on the horizon, but I wanted the kids to make the landfall, something they had been talking about for the past two days. After breakfast, I took Willie on deck and asked him if he could see anything off the starboard bow, for that's where the island ought to be. He squinted and said he couldn't see a thing. I told him to keep trying; St. Helena had to be out there. Finally he spotted it. "Landfall!" he shouted at the top of his lungs and jumped four feet in the air. Cathy rushed up on deck, looked out across the horizon, and hollered, "Landfall!" Then Gail, her hair in rollers, came up, took a look, and cried, "Landfall!" Finally I looked around to where Willie was pointing and said, "Landfall!" It was unanimous.

A cluster of peaks born of fire and thunder, St. Helena appeared serene and inviting as we approached. The kids were unwilling to lose sight of it for a minute, even when Gail announced that lunch was on the table. So she brought sandwiches on deck. But as often happens on picnics, clouds rolled in, and the island soon disappeared under a gray blanket. It was also a wet blanket, the squall dampening our spirits as well as wetting our appetizers. I asked for help with the main, but the call went unheeded. My crew had already scurried below.

In an hour the sun was out, and we were back in business. Swinging round to the lee side of the island, where the port of Jamestown was located, we furled the genoa, bagged headsails, and ran up ensign, courtesy flag, and burgee. Everything in proper order, I cranked the engine and motored into James Bay very casually, as though we had just been out for a day's sail. There was a yacht in the harbor that looked like *Sawankhaloke;* but that couldn't be, for she had three week's head start on *Molly Brown.* I pulled up beside her, and, sure enough, there was Claus, his bald head glinting in the sun, a can of beer in his hand.

Five minutes after I dropped the hook, a police

launch sped across the anchorage, and customs officer Eric Robb clutching a sheaf of papers came aboard. A big, likable Scot about my age, he welcomed us to fortress St. Helena. While I puzzled over the various forms, he and Gail chatted about things British. Divorced in England, he was, like Napoleon a century and a half earlier, living here in exile. But Eric's was self-imposed.

Willie pumped up the Avon, I grabbed a fifth of Johnny Walker, and we rowed over to *Sawankhaloke* for a courtesy call. The Danes had had a slow passage, as their boat was not very effective in headwinds. The snail's pace was frustrating to Claus, but it suited Maryrose just fine. For the first time on a boat, she hadn't gotten seasick. I introduced her to Willie, and they were soon swapping sea stories like a couple of old salts.

The two crews continued the reunion in the White House Inn except for Willie. He had to wait outside. No one questioned Kathy, but if they had, she was prepared to say she was 21. Right away I knew I was going to like Jamestown, picturesque as an English village. Nestled in a valley, with stucco houses clinging to the hillsides, it couldn't have changed much since Napoleon's day. Except for the beer, everything had to be 200 years old. Claus told us of a little restaurant in town. Anything you wanted, cooked to order, was available if requested three hours in advance. On the way back to the boat, I stopped there to leave word that *Molly Brown*'s crew would dine at seven. By that time everyone, especially Willie, was ready for the fried chicken, mashed potatoes with gravy, and hot bread set before us. I plunked a bottle of whiskey on the table and was just helping myself to a drink when Eric Robb walked in. After helping me drain the bottle, he invited us to his place for baths and a good night's sleep. The prospect of soaking in a hot tub was too tempting an offer to pass up, especially after 16 days at sea. It was midnight when we piled into Eric's police car and drove up the winding, rocky road to his home.

Eric fired up the ancient water heater with pine cones, explaining that although the thing was designed to burn charcoal, a scarce commodity on St. Helena, the cones served just as well. Besides, the island had plenty of pine trees. In a few minutes the parade to the tub began—Gail first, Cathy second, then Willie, and finally, at 2 A.M., me. When my turn came, I shoveled in more pine cones, acting on the assumption that three baths had used all the hot water. The fire blazing lustily, I drew my tub and stepped in. I had just finished the first verse of "Buttons and Bows" when the tank burst, flooding the bathroom. Eric, hearing the explosion, rushed to open the door, found it locked, put his shoulder to it, and crashed through, landing in the tub with me. In the confusion that followed I thought, this is like it must be on a torpedoed submarine. We mopped up the mess and went to bed.

Cathy and Willie, up with the morning sun, awakened me with their chattering outside my window. I quickly dressed, downed a glass of orange juice, and joined them in the yard. Eric had left instructions with his maid that breakfast should be served at 9:30. We had an hour to explore the old gun implacement just below the house. It was ideally situated, commanding the entire harbor from its high, rocky perch. Although the cannon had been removed, the fortification's gun rooms and quarters, carved in the rock, remained intact. As we groped through the dark, musty tunnels, it didn't take much to imagine British soldiers manning the premises, ready to blow anything out of the water flying French colors. We turned into one passageway, and what dim light remained soon faded. Inching forward, I put down a foot, felt nothing, and drew it back. I struck a match and found myself on the brink of a ladder well. I told Cathy to hang onto my shirt, and we would go back for a flashlight. "Willie," I said, "can you see the way out?" No answer. I thought he was behind Cathy. She did too. He must have taken another passage. Hugging the wall, we were feeling our way back when a blood-curdling scream froze me in my tracks. Willie had his clammy little fingers around Cathy's throat. She could have choked him.

At breakfast Eric said he was having a constable deliver us a car. It was a Hillman Imp left in his care by a schoolteacher friend vacationing in England. Gail, who had a British driver's license, was appointed chauffeur. That was the second job she had landed within a week. Watching me keep the log at sea, she had remarked: "I do not know why you keep that foolish thing when you cannot even read your own handwriting." I handed her the log. Her first entry read: "Island scenery is extremely attractive and quite beautiful in places—surprisingly green. Very hilly and the roads comprise a never-ending series of hairpin bends."

Wheeling around those bends, we set out in search of Longwood, Napoleon's last home. With commendable foresight, Gail had packed a lunch in case we got lost in the boondocks. We found Longwood atop a windy hill, where it commanded breathtaking views of the entire island. We parked in front of a picket fence—no other cars were around—and strolled through the well-kept gardens before entering the one-story, pink stucco house. Now a museum open to the public, it was filled with antique furnishings, fine silver, and paintings. If you have to go to jail, I thought, this is the way to go. With no airport to funnel travelers in, St. Helena gets few visitors.

Besides ourselves, there was only an elderly couple at Longwood, and for all I know, they might have been descendants of the Little Corporal. We concluded our pilgrimage by picnicking on Napoleon's lawn. Then back into the Hillman and down the hairpins to Napoleon's empty tomb (his bones now repose in Paris), with a side trip to the abandoned British fort on the highest part of the island. Standing on the parapet, we watch *Sawankhaloke*—as Gail poetically logged—"leaving in the light of the setting sun." She was bound for Ascension, and we soon would be.

We returned to Jamestown and met Eric at the Consular, the other pub in town. He was having a cold beer with a retired British merchant captain. They were discussing Waterloo. The captain laughed as he pondered what might have happened had Napoleon won. Maybe Wellington would have been exiled to some place like St. Helena. Well, the battle changed the course of history—no argument there. But what, I thought, had been the total gain? I would ask Willie when we got back to sea. He would know.

All hands slept late, and it was almost noon before we rowed in for another round of sightseeing. I stopped at the White Horse for a get-acquainted drink with sailors from the British tanker *Wave Chief.* Willie, spurning an invitation to go shopping with the girls, waited at the door. He soon discovered that he could meet as many interesting people on the outside as I could on the inside. When I emerged into the sunshine, he said: "Uncle Dickie, I met a man who wants to talk to you." He led me across the street to a keen-eyed old gentleman holding a package. He said I was to deliver it to America. I asked him what was in it. He opened the package and showed me a beautiful model of *La Salle* in a bottle. I told him it would be a pleasure to carry the mail once more for Hal Autenreith. And by the way, could he make a model of

Molly Brown? He could if he had a photograph of the boat. I didn't, but I had an artist who could provide him with a sketch. Gail was summoned from a nearby shop and did the drawing on the spot, Hasler and all. The old gentleman promised he would have the model bottled in two days.

Next morning I moved *Molly Brown* to the quay so we could take on water. While Gail prepared breakfast, Willie asked if he could go rowing in the Avon. I said sure but stay close to *Molly Brown.* Half an hour later I went up on deck to call him for breakfast. No Willie in sight. I had a good view of the harbor, and there wasn't anything there except *Wave Chief.* Willie had to be on the far side of the tanker, by the gangway, entertaining the crew. I told Gail we would eat and save something for Willie. By the time I finished my second cup of coffee I was getting worried. It wasn't like Willie to miss a meal. Back on deck for another look, I spotted *Wave Chief*'s launch heading for the quay. I motioned for the boatswain to come alongside. Was Willie over there in the rubber boat? No, he hadn't seen either one all morning. I explained the situation. He said climb in and we'll search the harbor.

After combing James Bay from one end to the other, the boatswain said we had better get more help. He swung around and gunned for the ship. "Hold it!" I yelled. A fishing boat coming in from the ocean had caught my eye—and it had a tow. As it closed I recognized the trailing dinghy. But where the hell was Willie? A minute later a voice rang out from the bridge deck. "Uncle Dickie!" Willie was jumping and waving his arms. Nothing this side of Hluhluwe moved in quite the same manner. For the first time in an hour my heart slowed to its normal beat.

Between bites of toast and jam, Willie told us what had happened. He was just rowing along, see, when this wind started blowing, and pretty soon he was way out in the middle of the bay. And, boy, was he getting scared. But it was kinda fun too. He tried to row against the wind and got so tired he thought his arms would fall off. Naw, he didn't cry, not much anyway, because he knew Uncle Dickie would figure out what happened and come looking for him in *Molly Brown.* And he would have found him too, if that man in the fishing boat hadn't seen him first. Boy, that's a keen boat; you never saw so much fishing stuff, miles of line and thousands of hooks and . . . Willie, I said, finish your breakfast.

That evening Gail and I had cocktails with Eric and *Wave Chief*'s skipper. I thanked the captain for the assistance his boatswain had given me. "I wish I had been in on it from the start," he remarked. "There's a light cruiser and a destroyer within 50 miles of the island. I could have radioed them, and we jolly well would have had some action around here for a change." Yes, I thought, and I jolly well would have gotten some action too if Willie had written his mother that he was lost at sea, and Uncle Dickie had to call in the British navy to hunt for him.

Tomorrow, Saturday, June 20, was departure day for *Molly Brown.* The captain insisted that my crew, especially Willie, join him for lunch in the officer's mess. Eric said he would be there. After completing a few last-minute chores—not the least of which was picking up *Molly Brown* under glass—we rowed over to *Wave Chief* shortly after noon. We were treated to a grand tour followed by cocktails and Chinese cuisine served by Indian messmen. Eric arrived bearing an object I had admired in his office—a yellowed old map of St. Helena. In one corner he had penned: "To the master and crew of *Molly Brown,* all the very, very best for the future."

We sailed at 4:45. As *Molly Brown* passed *Wave*

Chief, the captain ran up code flags, sending us a message. I could not read it.

Gail logged: "Dickie and Cathy hoist the mainsail at 1800 hours, then the genoa. We enjoy a good supper and retire to bed at 2200 hours." I told Gail she was doing a fine job—her penmanship certainly had mine beat by a country mile—but I had better keep the log at sea.

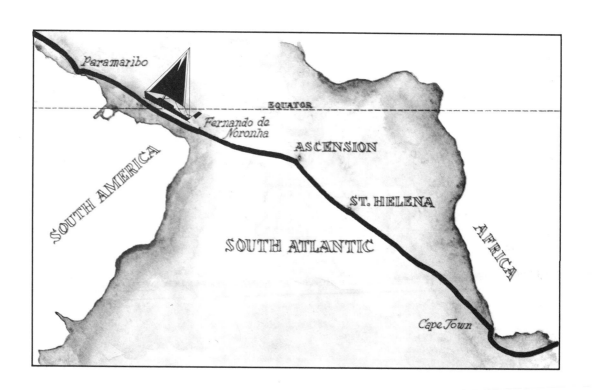

Chapter 14

Sunday, **June 21:**	Air is light out of the southeast, and *Molly Brown* is riding easy at four knots. After breakfast of lamb chops and fried eggs, Gail gives my back a rubdown. Ocean sailing does not have to be as bad as some people make it. At 1100 I fly the spinnaker—the first time it's been out of the bag since Tucker left. At dusk it comes down. Perfect sailing through the night.
Monday, **June 22:**	The chute is up again at 1000. Two nice flying fish have flung themselves aboard, and I clean them for lunch. *Molly Brown* becomes a floating bakery as Gail and Kathy spend the afternoon making chocolate chip cookies. Willie says he has tasted better, quits after the first dozen. The wind freshens at 1700, and I drop the spinnaker and pole out No. 1 genny.
Tuesday, **June 23:**	We fly the chute most of the day, but the Hasler cannot think fast enough to prevent it from collapsing. Cathy, Gail, and I take turns at the helm. Sunbathing in the afternoon. Steak and kidney pie out of a can for supper. The cabbage is fresh.
Wednesday, **June 24:**	I'm up early for a time tick. At 0800 I awaken Cathy with a spanking. Today is her fourteenth birthday. After Willie and Gail get in their licks, we try

for the third time to eat St. Helena bacon. The Chinese who sold it to Gail told her it would keep well at sea. A lump of almost solid salt, it would keep in the jungle. In a makeshift oven I fashioned from a tin bread box, Gail bakes a birthday cake, decorating it with pink candles she bought in Jamestown. Birthday dinner menu: steak smothered in onions and mushrooms, Brussels sprouts, mashed potatoes, red wine, cake. Gail lulls us to sleep reading horror stories.

Thursday, June 25:   Wind has backed to the east and is now abeam. A sun line at noon costs Cathy and me 25 cents apiece. We have a numbers game going, based on miles traveled from fix to fix. Gail wins with a guess of 120—right on the button. Good sailing all afternoon. Ham, beans, and beets for supper followed by another ghost story.

We made our landfall shortly after sunrise and were abeam of Ascension at 2 P.M. Rounding the leeward side, we gazed upon a great pile of brown volcanic ash studded with radio masts and radar domes. It looked like a big pincushion. We motored into Clarence Bay, and there was *Sawankhaloke* swinging at anchor half a mile from shore. I threw Annis a line and asked why the hell he had anchored way out here. He said you'll see in a minute, and I did. A big roller came in, and *Molly Brown* began to rise, slowly at first, then faster and higher as the huge swell went under her and crashed against the beach. Spray flew to the top of a 30-foot-high rock jetty, where a crane was gingerly lifting a Shell tank trailer from a rocking lighter. The crane operator had to be a former brain surgeon. I asked Annis if there wasn't an easier way to get ashore. He said not unless *Molly Brown* had wings and I flew her in. I thanked him and pumped up the Avon.

Gail and Cathy, with purses in hand and fresh hairdos, stepped into the dinghy as if going to a party.

Rowing in, I tried to figure out where to land. With each passing roller, I knew the beach was out of the question. Try that, and we would be somersaulted and washed ashore like dead fish. The only alternative was the jetty. How we would get to the top of it I didn't know; perhaps the crane would pluck us out of the water. As we neared the rock-ribbed structure, a workman on high pointed to a ladder. The task now was to step out of the Avon and onto the ladder—not as simple as it sounds, for the rubber boat rose and fell in the swells like a runaway elevator. Two men came part way down the steps to lend a hand as we disembarked. Gail went first, and a roller was a close second, wetting her from the waist down before the two men could pull her out of range. Cathy was next. Same results. Willie scrambled up without a drop touching him. I got a bath. The burly crane operator laughed so hard tears streamed down his face. He removed his hard hat, wiped his brow, and said, "That's about it, pal. Three outta four you're gonna get it." Then he burst out laughing again.

I was thinking how much fun it would be to knock his ass off the jetty when a hand tapped me on the shoulder. I turned to face the cold blue stare of Jeff Appleby, a man of my size and build, clad in British tropicals, rows of medals stretched across his chest, swagger stick in hand. By God, I thought, General Montgomery himself. "I assume you are the captain," he sneered. "No," I replied, water dripping into my shoes, "that short guy is. I'm the tailgunner." We spent the next three minutes staring at each other, and work on the quay came to a standstill. Nobody wanted to miss the fight. They were disappointed, but not by much. Appleby demanded to see my security clearance. I told him I had none. He pointed his swagger stick to the ocean. "Leave!" he barked. I told him we weren't budging until we had taken on fuel and fresh water. While he was thinking up another command, Gail moved in and started talking to him in British. I walked over to the crane and sat down on the track. "He's a real son of a bitch," commented the hard hat. "You don't say," I said.

Gail won us a reprieve, Appleby agreeing to let us stay until we got water. The crane operator, a redneck from Tennessee, turned out to be a hell of a nice fellow. He told me where to find a store and volunteered to help with the water next day. We hiked up the volcanic ash trail to Georgetown, which isn't a town at all but a collection of Quonset huts unrelieved by a blade of grass or a single tree. If there ever was a nowheresville, this was it. I found the store and bought a pack of beer and a quart of ice cream. Standing outside in our drip-dries, we satisfied thirsts and appetites. As Gail handed me another cold one, we saw a trail of dust streaming over the hill and down the road toward us. "It's got to be the bloody American Indians," she declared. She was half right; there was an American behind all that grit—and a blue '69 Chevrolet, U.S. Air Force in gold on the door. Out stepped Major Jack Conch, base commander. There was one decent spot on this island, he said; away we roared in another cloud of dust.

The officers' club was small, nice, and well stocked. I told Jack about my encounter with Appleby, adding that I probably should apologize to the guy now that I had cooled off. Jack said Appleby wasn't a bad sort, just leery of uninvited guests. He still remembered the last yacht that called—one captained by a woman. I've heard of her, I said. The trouble, he continued, started right here in the club, at that shuffleboard table. She was playing one of her crew, and he beat her. And that made her sore, I interrupted. That it did, he assured me. She picked up the deckhand by the seat of his pants and slung the poor fellow down the length of the board. He crashed into the scoring apparatus at the end of the table. Lights blinked, bells rang. Since the fellow was still breathing, madam captain decided to give him a return trip. Before she could get her hands on him, the rest of her crew stepped in. It was a laudable act of mercy that she interpreted as an act of mutiny. The fight was on. M.P.'s were called, but decided not to interfere since it was a civil and not a military disturbance. Appleby's forces were then summoned, and the captain was thrown into the clink—not, however, without a struggle. When her boat was provisioned, she was kicked off the island and told never to return. Then, Jack laughed, you had to show up with a chip on your shoulder.

Dinner with Jack was followed by drinks and sea stories with the crew of *Sawankhaloke.* I do not remember how we got back to *Molly Brown.* I do know that a sober man would never have dared those rollers in the middle of the night. There must be a moral there somewhere, and if I figure out what it is, I'll drop it in later.

Next morning I threw the laundry bag into the Avon and, tossing caution to the winds, soloed to the beach. The dinghy landed first, then me upside down with a mouthful of salt water; lastly, the laundry bag washed up. I hoofed into town and, after disposing of the laundry, paid a call on Appleby. We chatted a bit, shook hands, and that was that. I breakfasted with Jack in the officers' club. A fellow by the name of Storrs joined us, and before I knew what was taking place, I was being shanghied to Boatswain Bird Island as a member of a scientific expedition. Storrs, an ornithologist, had to go over there and collect a few birds for the Smithsonian Institution. Jack had been asked to lend all possible assistance—and that's where I came in. The only way to get to Boatswain

Bird Island, off the eastern tip of Ascension, was by boat. And the only boats in the harbor—as Jack ticked them off—were the lighters, which were in use; *Sawankhaloke,* which had no motor, and *Molly Brown.* Major, are you trying to tell me something? Now that I had volunteered, he said, I was entitled to the details. He would supply box lunches and beer; I would contribute the boat. The expedition would consist of ourselves, two scuba divers (to investigate the sea life around the island), Storrs's assistant, my crew, and *Sawankhaloke*'s. I reminded Jack that *Molly Brown* was a 35-foot sailboat, not a boxcar. He said we would just have to squeeze everybody on.

The expedition got underway at noon. The two cooks from *Sawankhaloke,* Maryrose and Daughter, signed on, but not the Danes. They wanted no part of this folly. Two hours and several cases of beer later, we were anchored off Boatswain Bird Island, a barren hunk of rock that only a sooty tern could love. Jack, Storrs, his assistant, and I made up the assault party. A snorkeler manned the Avon. In case I should be lost, Willie would be responsible for getting the girls to the States. Since there was no beach to hit, we maneuvered the rubber boat under a rope that dangled from a ledge. After pulling ourselves over this obstacle, it was all uphill. I brought up the rear—by necessity, not choice—grasping for handholds in rock of about the consistency of caked brown sugar. Ahead—or to be more precise, overhead—rose 300 feet of the crumbly stuff. Below, of course, lay the Atlantic Ocean, with the rocky ledge to break my fall if I should slip, which at H-hour plus 10 minutes I thought was imminent. Now, when I was 12 years old there wasn't a tobacco barn in Prince Georges County too high for me to scale; and when I was 21 I was jumping out of airplanes in the 101st Airborne. So heights don't bother me. Not much. I was stretched out like a snake, with every finger and toe dug into the crumbly rock, when Jack returned to see what was holding me up. "What's wrong with you?" he inquired. "I'm scared, goddam it! Can't you see how far down it is to the ocean?" He grabbed me by the hand and helped me over the grade. Hand in hand, we made it to the top where the rock plateaued. Birds were as thick as chickens in a broiler house. You had to scuffle them out of the way to walk through. There were terns, boobies, frigate birds puffing out their red pouches, and I don't know how many other species. But Storrs did. Hopping from one feathered flock to another, he was wringing necks as fast as I could shuck oysters, his friend at his heels stuffing the specimens into plastic bags. Actually, Stores wasn't wringing necks. I just put that in for shock value. He had a more sophisticated method, pressing the innocent creatures in a certain fashion to make their lungs collapse. They died in his embrace, so to speak. Storrs thinned the flock by maybe a couple of dozen birds, insignificant when you consider there must have been half a million on the rock. I couldn't prove it, but I would be willing to bet there were more birds there when we left than when we arrived. Eggs were hatching all over the place.

I won't bore you with details of the trip down. It will suffice to say that all my shirt buttons had been scraped off and my fingernails didn't need trimming. After a swim to wash off the guano, sweat, and tears, the assault group climbed aboard *Molly Brown* and proceeded to empty the beer chest. The girls were frying fish impaled by the spear-wielding scuba duo. The pair had also boated a sea turtle, now lying on its back in the cockpit. Mission accomplished, we hurried to the harbor lest we be late for the dance. Jack had invited one and all to the monthly Ascension Island ball.

With more officers' quarters than officers to fill them, Jack had room to spare for guests. We showered and changed in G.I. bathrooms, piled into the blue Chevy—a lunar landing vehicle would have been more appropriate—and bounced past craters and piles of ash to the top of Rocky Hill, site of Ascension Island Club. Willie didn't make the trip because he was too tired and too young. The crew of *Sawankhaloke* did, however, which pleased Jack, for he was anxious to get better acquainted with Daughter. Claus, who already knew her pretty well and didn't fancy sharing the wealth, was there, doubtless to dance, but also to see that Jack didn't monopolize all of Daughter's time. She was a most attractive girl. As things turned out, both were lucky to get one dance each with her. Packed with American airmen, satellite tracking station people, employees of British Cable and Wireless, Appleby's staff, Pan American personnel, and local citizens, men outnumbered women by a good twenty to one. As Gail logged: "the dance was great fun if exhausting for all the girls, who, due to an acute shortage of females, virtually danced nonstop." I spent most of the evening talking to Claus, who spent most of the evening keeping an eye on Jack.

At 4 A.M. we migrated down to the beach like a bunch of lemmings, stopping at the barracks to collect Rip Van Willie. Captain Claus, with a fine disdain for the relentless rollers licking at his feet, surveyed the inky domain and, seeing nothing and fearing nothing, ordered his crew into his leaky, wooden dinghy. "I will row through the surf to my boat," he proclaimed, and spat into the wind. He was drunk—but who wasn't?—and, worse, intoxicated with the desire to prove his prowess to fair Daughter. I thought it was a strange way to display one's courage, comparable to jumping off a building into a tub of water. Claus and his obedient crew were lucky. The first roller capsized the boat and washed all hands ashore without inflicting permanent injury. Claus said he would sleep on the beach before he would go through that again.

Now it was my turn to play the gallant. I told Gail and the kids to return to barracks; I was sleeping on *Molly Brown* this night. Loyal to the last one of them, they vowed to follow me to the end of the earth—at least to the end of the jetty. And there we repaired; then down the ladder and into the faithful Avon. We hit it on the way up and rode it on the way down, with nary a salty drop spilling into the boat. In thirty minutes we were snug in our bunks. It was then, as I drifted off, that the moral I was seeking came to me. It was: If you can't join 'em, beat 'em.

I slept till noon. When I awoke, Cathy was at the stern with a loaf of bread and a spear the scuba divers had left behind. As little black fish circled the bait, Cathy thrust, missing every time. Jack was on the jetty waving. At the dance he suggested we make an excursion to the farm at the top of Green Mountain—not for science, just for the hell of it. Besides ourselves, the party would include the scuba divers, my crew, and Daughter—whom, I suspect, was the inspiration for the mountain madness. I rounded up crew, picked up Daughter, and headed for the steps. Only two of us got drenched, which, considering the odds, was a victory for our side. The blue Chevy— otherwise known as Air Force One—and an Air Force pickup were waiting for us. Willie jumped into the pickup and planted himself between the scuba guys, whose names were either John and Paul or Dan and Dale. Just a minute; I'll check the log and see if Gail noted the names. Yep. Ray, Dan, and Dale. Whatever the names and numbers, we caravanned up the winding road past Lady Hill Drip and God Be Thanked Tank to about the 2,000-foot height, where the road played out. As we walked to the top, bumping our heads against the clouds, I suggested to Jack that we turn around and go back. He said why? And I said I think I'm going to throw up—or, in this case, down. Well, he said, that's too bad but we can't turn back now; Willie has gone on ahead to the bamboo forest with John and Paul. Onward and upward we trudged, and I began having hallucinations. I thought I saw cows grazing on the side of the mountain, which was covered with grass instead of lava. They didn't fall off, I reasoned, because they had twice as many legs as I had, and besides, that would have ruined the hallucination. Jack, waiting as I caught up, remarked: "Quite a nice dairy herd they have up here." "You mean they're real?" I said.

In a very literal sense, the top of Green Mountain is a little piece of England. English topsoil, brought as ballast in British bottoms, was hauled up the mountain by donkeys and spread upon the barren summit. Nourished by alpine showers, crops took root in the soil; grass inched down the slopes; a few imported cattle, pigs, and chickens gained a foothold. Now, after a century and more of soil-building, there are some 70 or 80 productive acres. We filed past farm buildings and greenhouse up to the bamboo forest, which reminded me of a corn field. Don't miss it if you go to Ascension. At the very top of the mountain was a tunnel, like the eye in a needle. Back when the British were over-reacting to the presence of their prisoner on St. Helena, they fortified Ascension, planting a sentry post on the peak. The tunnel was cut through so the lookouts wouldn't have to go over the top or around the mountain to report that the French fleet was coming. They used it either for that or as a place to get out of the rain and have a smoke. Cathy and Gail were scared to walk through it. I couldn't understand why; I never heard of anybody falling out

210

of a tunnel.

"The descent was even more precarious, and great screams are heard as various members of the party fall muddily on their bottoms." So Gail recorded in the log, after our visit to the pig pen. We hairpinned down the mountain to pizzas and beer in the officers' club. Jack wanted to chat. His situation was somewhat like mine—same age, divorced, getting away from things awhile—and I guess you could say he was on the make too. Divorced guys usually are. He liked Daughter a lot and had asked her to stay— without benefit of clergy, I presume—and she was considering the proposition. "Uncle Dickie," he asked, "what do you think?" "Major," I replied, "I have no thoughts on the matter. The worst thing I could do would be to give advice—not that you would take it, but it might influence you in some way." He said I should run for Congress.

Two things of note happened the following day, Monday, June 29. Daughter decided to stay with *Sawankhaloke,* which made Claus happy and Jack as blue as Air Force One. The second item was a bit more complex: The two boats took on water, and in *Molly Brown*'s case, gas, under frightful conditions. The rollers and pounding surf were so bad that the lighters had stopped shuttling and the crane was moved back 30 feet. Nevertheless, both Claus and I were determined to go to sea, particularly Claus who was reluctant to linger much longer lest Daughter changed her mind. Since the wooden dinghy would have been smashed to splinters on the jetty, we ferried the water out to the boats in the Avon, averaging, I would estimate, one capsize for each gallon delivered. We finished at 2 P.M. after six hours without food or drink. Now the difficult part began—getting 20 gallons of gas aboard *Molly Brown.* There was one so-called gas station on the island, and it closed at noon. I called the owner and begged him to open up for ten minutes. He told me to come back in the morning; he was busy. I told him I was sailing tonight, and he said why didn't you say so? We had almost filled one jerry jug when his pump ran dry. I paid him for five gallons, thanked him for his trouble, and called Jack. He brought down a 50-gallon drum in the trunk of Air Force One. We siphoned off enough to fill the cans and cussed them out to the boat. It was now five o'clock. Jack's bribe of hamburgers, showers, and G.I. beds was snapped up by the crew. Besides, there was a party at a British couple's place. Okay, we'll leave tomorrow. Claus decided to do the same. He would see us at the party. He was feeling pretty sure of himself.

While dancing with Maryrose that night, I asked her if she had any regrets. She said she didn't. Oh, the Danes were a little on the yachty side, but that didn't bother her. And she and Daughter got along all right. We reminisced awhile about the good old days on Makatea, Tahiti, Bali. Maryrose, I said, let's change the subject before I start crying. She laughed, and in a few minutes was dancing with someone else.

The party broke up about four in the morning. Gail and Cathy returned to Air Force quarters, and I rowed out to *Molly Brown.* Whenever I needed a distraction—which I did that night, for the rollers were bigger than ever—I would try to solve the oar mystery. The Avon had identical hard-rubber oar locks, and the wooden oars were just alike. What mystified me was that one oar was badly worn at the oar lock while the other oar hardly showed any wear at all. Maybe Willie would know why.

Jack brought Willie and the girls down to the jetty about ten o'clock. Handshakes and goodbyes, a tear in Daughter's eye, and the two crews were ready to sail. We motored around *Sawankhaloke* as she

weighed anchor and shook out her sails. She was
steering 290 compass for Recife; *Molly Brown*'s
heading was 310 for Barbados, more than 3,000 miles
away. I set the main and the big genoa. At dusk
Sawankhaloke was two miles off our stern, but the gap
was steadily widening as our courses diverged. Willie
and I sat in the cockpit and watched her kerosene
running lights gradually diminish. Finally they
disappeared, and all we could see were the stars.
Willie, I said, I've got a little mystery for you. It's about
those oars . . .

Annapolis

Morehead City

ATLANTIC OCEAN

Miami

CUBA

GREAT INAGUA

HISPANIOLA

ST. THOMAS

CARIBBEAN SEA

BARBADOS

Paramaribo

SOUTH AMERICA

Chapter 15

**Wednesday,
July 1:**
    I get up at 0900 and set the ship's clock back an hour. *Molly Brown* self-steered well all night under the main and No. 1 genny. We will stay with that as long as the breeze holds steady out of the south. I start *Guns of Navarrone* in the afternoon. A star fix doesn't work out. I must be out of practice.

**Thursday,
July 2:**
    Better luck with the stars at 0500. Omelet, marmalade, and English muffins for breakfast. Sun line at noon puts us 235 miles out of Ascension—fair mileage. I read until dinner. Wind freshens at 2100, and I drop the main.

**Friday,
July 3:**
    Clear and warm. I get a morning sun line and jot the numbers down on back of an envelope. Self-steerer won't work when I hoist the main, so I take the tiller. Absent-mindedly I crumple the envelope and toss it overboard. I can't get a noon sun line, and clouds prevent an evening fix, spoiling our guessing game on miles covered. Person with poorest guess washes the supper dishes. Girls claim I lose today by default.

**Saturday,
July 4:**
    Four days out and 2500 miles to go—time to make a decision. We can run straight for Barbados

and risk getting stalled in the doldrums, or we can attempt to skirt most of them by heading for the Brazilian coast above the Amazon, then ride a favorable current up the continental shelf for a thousand miles. I worry with the charts all day and finally choose the long route. Those doldrums scare me. After a fine spaghetti dinner, we celebrate the Fourth by using up the rest of the shotgun shells on tin cans tossed off the stern.

Sunday, July 5:
After coffee I wing out No. 2. *Molly Brown* is flying. A noon sight gives us 185 miles for the day. With that kind of mileage, I don't mind washing dishes. After lunch I hoist the main to get more northing; otherwise, we might end up in Recife with the Danes. Willie hooks a fish and loses it. The girls sunbathe. I take a nap. After dinner Cathy entertains us with card tricks.

Monday, July 6:
I pole out the genoa to run down wind, and a halyard snaps. At 1000 we're becalmed. And hot. But we should be; we're getting closer to the equator. A noon fix tells me we have made only 20 miles since yesterday—a lousy run. I am awakened from my afternoon nap by two tomcats fighting. Or a reasonable facsimile. Gail is insisting that Willie take a bath, and he is refusing. He has not had a bath in a week she says. Neither have I, so I can silently sympathize with Willie. Sponging off in the cockpit with salt water that won't lather doesn't get you all that clean; besides, the soap clings to you like adhesive from an old Band-Aid. Personally, I prefer to wait for rain and get a fresh-water bath. But Gail is hard-nosed about bathing whether needed or not; and, as captain, I have to back her up to preserve discipline. I order Willie to bathe. He says he won't because the salt water makes his skin itch. I look at Gail, and she says bathe. I look at Willie, and he says no. Impasse. I recess the hearing until tomorrow morning over Gail's

objections. But, hell, I can't spank the kid when I'm just as guilty as he. At dinner adversaries trade dirty looks, no pun intended.

Tuesday, July 7: Lying in my bunk, I decide the only suitable punishment for Willie is to confine him to quarters for the day. I roll out at 0900 for breakfast, request Gail send the boy in for sentencing. She can't; he's on deck without any clothes on. It's been raining since daybreak. God looks after small children. Willie towels off, dresses, hands me the soap. I get the message. It pours all day, and we fill the tanks from the rain catch. Gail dons foul-weather gear and takes the midnight watch. We are back in the shipping lanes.

Wednesday, July 8: Gail awakens me at 0100 to inform me the other genny halyard had broken. Lightning *does* strike twice. I run the genoa up on the spinnaker halyard. Now we can't carry double headsails until we rove a new halyard through the masthead block. That means someone has to ride the boatswain chair to the top of the mast, and it can't be me; I'm too heavy for the girls to hoist 35 feet. Cathy could do it in a dead calm. I'm back in the sack at 0300 and up at seven for an early sunline. Cherry crumble for lunch and a noon shot. We're 125 miles east of Fernando de Noronha, a tiny archipelago off the northeast tip of Brazil. We will go in there for repairs. Sight two ships, decide to stand watch through the night.

Thursday, July 9: Morning star fix puts us 35 miles out. Landfall at 1000. We round the southwest point, sail up close to shore, and drop the launch hook. Sailing Directions say the island is inhabited, but all we can see are palm trees. I tie two spare halyards to Cathy's belt and winch her up on the main reel. One rope tail hits the deck. A few minutes later Cathy drops the other. Job well done.

The next entry in the log reads: "We go for a swim and depart 1600." Let me elaborate. To begin with, I had told the crew that under no circumstances were we going ashore. I knew far too well what was likely to happen. You walk on the beach, you meet some perfect stranger who says, "I know you can't stay, but before you go, you must see my pet dinosaur." You're trapped. My crew didn't say a word; they just stood on the bow and stared at the inviting sand. All right. You can swim ashore. I'm not pumping up the rubber boat. Splash! With me right behind. We played on the beach for an hour and would have played longer had not a Tarzan roar boomed down from a cliff. Three black figures were silhouetted against the sky. I said let's get the hell out of here. Gail said don't be afraid; I'm quite sure they are friendly. That's what I was afraid of. Back to the log.

Cathy cooks dinner. Willie wants to stand watch. I ask him if he can stay awake. Try me, he says. He takes it from 2100 to midnight, Cathy following, Gail finishing the night. Proper captains do not stand watches.

Friday, July 10:
Pouring down rain, and nothing wrong with that. We need another bath. Cathy catches first fish since leaving Cape Town—a nice dolphin. We have it for lunch. After poling out No. 2 genny, I read Robert Ruark's *Horn of the Hunter.* Rest of the dolphin for dinner. Cathy takes first watch.

Saturday, July 11:
Gail wakes me 0330 to stand watch. Clear, lovely night to go sailing. No ships in sight. I get a sun line at 0800, another at noon—165-mile run. We catch another fish, have it for dinner, then listen to bossa nova on the radio.

Sunday, July 12:
Gail makes omelet and pancakes for breakfast. Noon sight shows another good run of 165 miles. We're in the coastal current. Wing and wing in the afternoon, and we're logging knots.

Monday, July 13:
We're approaching the equator, and I've alerted Willie to look for a yellowish line in the water.

"I see it!" he shouts, and I tell him that's just about where it ought to be. Wind freshens in the afternoon, and I drop the main. Cathy bakes cookies. Star fix with moon and Venus is unsatisfactory.

Tuesday, July 14: I hoist main at 0900, as southeasterly drops to a steady force three. Good evening fix puts us 1165 miles out of Barbados.

Thursday, July 16: Wednesday was great sailing, and today begins the same way. I set the chute. Becalmed at 1400, we take a swim. Cathy screams, "Shark!" and we scramble up the ladder. She says it swam right up to her face mask. I tell her that's because it wanted to see if she was good-looking. She doesn't think that's funny. I don't either, really. We motor until 2300, when a breeze comes in out of the northeast.

Friday, July 17: Wind veers east at 0200, and I reset the Hasler. After breakfast, I hoist the main and spinnaker. A rusty old coaster steams past us at noon, says hello with a blast of its horn. Willie aims his Instamatic. Current is changing color—from blue to muddy. Must be the outflow of the Amazon. Becalmed again. I drop the spinnaker at 2000 and start the engine.

Saturday, July 18: Hot, muggy, and low on fuel. Apprentice helmsman Willie asks what we will do when the tank runs dry. I tell him we will sit out here and flop until a breeze comes in. But, he says, what if one doesn't come in? He's got a point. Should we detour to Surinam? Unanimous for yes. One problem: I have no chart of the coast. My Atlantic Ocean chart, however, provides some help. It indicates there's a lightship with a radio beacon at the mouth of the Surinam River. Twelve miles up the river is Paramaribo, the capital and our gas station. Rain clouds at 1400 stir up a light southeast breeze, and I set the chute. By 1700 we're motoring again.

Sunday, July 19: I take the watch at 0100, see fishing boats. They must be working fairly close to shore; I can smell land.

Molly Brown sputters twice and cuts off. The tank is dry. We have one five-gallon jerry canful left, but that's for the river. I crawl into my bunk and wait for daylight. Clouds thicken before dawn, so no fix. But we should be able to see land. A noon sight tells me we are 30 miles off the coast; we're not as close as I thought. A slight breeze comes in, and we work toward shore. Cathy spends the afternoon baking cookies, and Willie gets in the act with a pan of hot biscuits. Ouch. I dropped one on my foot. Still no landfall at 1600, and no radio beacon on the RDF. I take it up onto the cabin top. Ten minutes later I get a weak signal. The breeze picks up, the beacon grows louder. When the sun goes down, it should silhouette the coast. The sun goes down, and still no landfall. What the hell? The water is chocolate brown and, I suspect, shallow. I use the depth finder for the first time since I don't know when, and it registers ten feet. I toss the lead line over. Two fathoms, and a lead line doesn't lie. We're going to look like yokels in the morning—hard up on the mud and yelling landfall. I drop the sails, drop the anchor, and go to bed wondering where the hell we are.

At six o'clock the next morning, it was all too clear; we were in the middle of a vast marsh, the tallest object around being weeds. I turned on the RDF and, as you might have guessed, the signal came in loud and clear from across the mud flats. Since *Molly Brown* wasn't an airboat, I saw two possibilities: go up the coast or down the coast. I poured the last five gallons into the tank and cranked the engine. Cathy, at the tiller, asked for a heading. I said up. It was a good guess. The light ship came into view in half an hour, and there was the river, the muddiest in the world, without a doubt. I switched on the RDF, and the radio signal was not coming from the lightship, but from up the river. Somebody had moved the damned transmitter. That explained why we had tried to sail across the mud flats.

Now all we had to do was find the channel. As we fought a good five-knot current, a shrimp trawler churned up behind us, and I began wondering how to say "Which way to Paramaribo?" in Spanish. The diesel throttled back as the shrimper pulled alongside. "Hey, man," came the greeting from a laughing black face, "you lost or something?" He motioned for us to follow. On her stern was painted *Betty Sue,* Miami, Florida. We were getting closer to that green grass all the time.

There was no room at the dock, so we tied up beside *Betty Sue.* Customs officials came aboard and said we needed an agent. Few yachts come here, for obvious reasons, and when they do, they're treated like commercial vessels. Enter tall, thin, graying Jim Healy, agent for most U.S. traffic in Surinam. In ten minutes he had our papers in order and was escorting us to his station wagon. A native New Yorker who had been here for 20 years, he insisted on showing us around. Paramaribo is a bustling port city, although more typcial of the eighteenth century than the twentieth. True, it has a Reynolds aluminum plant and a dam the goverment is proud of, but everything else is old, wooden, and Dutch Colonial, a reminder that Surinam used to be called Dutch Guiana. We had cocktails at Jim's house, met his family, then joined them for dinner at a Chinese restaurant, where we had a few more drinks. Ordinarily, I'm a taciturn sort, but the liquor had loosened my tongue. "Jim," I said, for the fifteenth time, "that's the muddiest damned river I've ever seen in my life." I also said something else— "yes," when he invited us on a bus tour into the bush tomorrow. And I had planned to leave tonight.

Early next morning I gassed up *Molly Brown* while the girls did some shopping. I also checked with the captain of the shrimp boat to find out when the current ebbed. Seven o'clock that evening, he said. I was determined not to miss it.

We boarded the bus and rattled off into the bush, an Indian village our destination. Living in grass huts and running around naked, the tribesmen didn't have anything to be proud of except their pride, and that they were mighty proud of. I aimed my camera once; that was enough. It almost set off a riot. These people don't like to be photographed. I wouldn't either if I didn't have any clothes on. We got back to Paramaribo in one piece but dehydrated. Jim and I administered first-aid with a couple of cold ones; then it was time to go. As we stepped across the trawler, the captain handed me a present—a ten-pound box of frozen shrimp.

I took the helm and motored out into Old Muddy. Willie had a sandwich and almost fell asleep eating it. Tired out from sightseeing, he was in the sack before the sun went down. Cathy was too, but for a different reason. She had the midnight watch; and I wanted her to sleep now so she would be wide awake then. I told Gail to fry up enough shrimp for four people, since I was hungry enough for three. When they were ready, I cut off the engine and let *Molly Brown* drift with the current. It seemed safe enough. Her navigation lights were on, the river was wide and empty, and the current couldn't go anywhere but the ocean. I opened a bottle of wine, and we had a feast.

While lifting my glass for a final swallow, its contents suddenly flew into my face. Dishes crashed at my feet. The boat, after the initial hard shock, trembled like a plucked guitar string. I knew in an instant what had happened: A ship had plowed into us; water would soon start pouring in. Half stunned, I sat there a few seconds waiting for the boat to break apart and thinking what a fool I had been. When we didn't sink right away, I assumed we had merely run aground. I dashed up on deck and was immediately knocked down, felled by a tree limb. Nothing serious—just a flesh wound. I struggled to my feet and requested that a flashlight be passed up. Next I called for the saw. Willie, who was awake by this time, found it behind my bunk and brought it up. Cathy, who was also awake by this time, was right behind him with her Instamatic. A flash bulb popped. "They are not going to believe this at home," she said. "I don't even believe it."

We were in the jungle. There were trees behind us, in front of us, and on both sides. Branches were tangled in the rigging. Leaves covered the deck—and here I was without a rake. I climbed into the rigging and started sawing. Gail organized a cleanup detail. In an hour we had most of the debris cleared away. Then came the ticklish part—manuevering *Molly Brown* back into the river. I started the engine and we started to move, scraping past one tree, bouncing off another. Fortunately, the wooded point we had strayed onto was sufficiently flooded to give us keel room. Another hour and we were out of the woods. Once past the lightship, I set the Hasler and crawled into my bunk. It was 2 A.M.

Wednesday, July 22:

I awaken at 0800 to find Gail and the kids scrubbing the deck. It looks like it's covered with blood. Last night we had been trampling on inky red berries from off the trees. By nightfall the boat is reasonably clean, and the sea is calm. We start motoring.

Thursday, July 23:

Still under power. We have hit a stretch of the doldrums, but that's no problem; the tanks are full. Gail makes pizza for lunch, and I shoot the sun. We are 345 miles out of Barbados. A whisper of a breeze at 1900. I hoist the main and No. 1, but it isn't worth the effort. Back to power at 2100.

223

Friday, July 24: Hot and still. We lay under the awning, stop for a swim, count the miles. Kids are a little homesick. I tell them we will call home when we get to Barbados.

Saturday, July 25: I take the watch at zero hours. Not a breath of air. After breakfast a breeze. It's about time. I hoist No. 1 genny and main, and we reach toward Barbados. The genny tears. I drop it and raise No. 3. Hell, I could use my handkerchief now. We've got it made.

I saw shore lights at 0330 next morning. About nine I dropped the hook in Georgetown harbor and waited for customs. Before us rose the Holiday Inn. We stood on deck gazing at it as if we had never seen anything like it before. Investigating its attractions would come soon enough; right now, foremost in everyone's mind was mail. The kids had posted letters from every port since leaving Cape Town, and they were expecting a haul. They got it. Every member of the crew received letters except me. Not even a note from Internal Revenue.

We stayed in Barbados four days, which were probably three too many, and did all the touristy things, one of which was paying eight dollars for the worst meal I ever turned my nose up at. The steak, besides being about half the size of my baked potato, was as tough as rubber and about as tasty. Cathy called her parents and turned down their invitation to fly home. Willie was with me all the way too. I called Boots and asked her to send Kyle and Richard. They could meet us in St. Thomas, Virgin Islands, our next stop. She said no. I told her to think about it; I would call her again in St. Thomas. We provisioned the boat, picked up our laundry, and sailed the afternoon of the twenty-ninth on a fresh breeze.

Richard III

Thursday, July 30: Up at 0800, I spot what I think is St. Lucia, and hold course northerly to transit St. Lucia channel. At 1500 I realize the island is Martinique. Not very good navigating, but no harm done. We bear off between

Martinique and Dominica, turn the corner, and by dusk we are in the Leewards. At 2400 we see the lights of Guadeloupe.

Friday, July 31: Our breeze moderates at 0600, and I let Willie take a turn at the tiller. We sight Montserrat after lunch. Noon sight says we have 185 miles to go. Beef stew for dinner.

Saturday, August 1: Hazy morning. Can't get a noon latitude, but a radio bearing positions us 50 miles from St. Thomas. With no chart of the island, we have trouble working our way in. I cruise around till dusk, finally identify Frenchcap Cay. That's as far as we go. Will heave to for the night.

We were up and underway early Sunday morning, tying at the customs dock before eight o'clock. Paper work done, I moved *Molly Brown* to an anchorage at the St. Thomas Yacht Club and headed for the nearest telephone. I had thought up a hundred arguments why Boots should send the kids down here; maybe she would buy one—if she would answer the phone. After trying several times, I called Billy. He said that Boots had mentioned something about taking Kyle and Richard to the beach for the weekend. I walked back to the boat feeling pretty dejected. It was too early in the day to get drunk so I lay on my bunk and took a nap. My crew stayed behind, wolfing hot dogs and hamburgers at the grill in the marina.

It was about one o'clock when a breathless Willie shook me awake. "Uncle Dickie," he shouted, "quick! Come up on deck." I couldn't imagine what had gone wrong, and Willie didn't hang around to tell me. In about two seconds I was topside. There stood Gail, Cathy, Willie; the boat seemed to be in good shape. Okay. What's the joke? There was no joke. Coming alongside was a launch, with a couple of kids waving madly and shouting, "Daddy!" I reached over and hugged Kyle and Richard aboard. Everybody was talking at once. Boots and her husband Bobby Warfield just stood there and grinned. They had flown in Friday with the kids, thought it would be a nice surprise. I couldn't have wished for a better one.

Now my crew numbered six, which was about *Molly Brown*'s capacity. After several delightful days on St. Thomas, marred only by a broken heart, we were ready to sail. The broken heart belonged to Cathy, who had fallen in love. It is pure hell to fall in love when you are fourteen, but everybody does it. And it didn't do Cathy any good for me to tell her she would soon forget the guy and meet another she liked better. I didn't understand. Maybe not. Nevertheless, she did not jump ship; and on Wednesday, August 5, we said goodbye to Boots and Bobby, then set a northwestward course for Great Inagua Island, our last stop before Miami.

Thursday, August 6: Gail makes pancakes for breakfast, but Cathy isn't hungry. Kyle helps with the dishes. Willie and Richard are fishing. I shoot a sun line; 390 miles to Great Inagua. Cathy wants to be alone, sunbathes (and sobs) in her new bikini all day on the cabin top. Nice sailing under the main and No. 1 genoa. Cathy, sunburned around the waist, joins us for dinner. I think she is making a quick recovery.

Friday, August 7: Nice easterly, and *Molly Brown* is moving. I tune in for weather report from Coast Guard. Nothing to worry about. Richard has a loose tooth, which Willie volunteers to pull. Richard declines. Kyle throws out a line after lunch and, just like that, hooks a five-pounder. I don't know what kind, but we have it for dinner with fried potatoes. Cathy takes the first watch.

Saturday, August 8: At 0100 I jibe to get more northing and keep us well away from Hispaniola. Gail takes the watch at 0300, wakes me an hour later as *Molly Brown* is becalmed and drifting toward shore. I start the engine and get us back out into deep water. We motor all morning, and I put up the awning. A breeze comes in after lunch. Up goes the main and genny. Spaghetti for dinner, but no wine. The last time I had a glass of wine all hell broke loose. At midnight our easterly freshens, clouds roll in. We batten down for a squall.

Sunday, August 9: The squall didn't amount to much. Clear skies at daybreak. At 0800 I hoist the main and spinnaker. An hour later we sight Great Inagua. While working into Man of War Bay, the spinnaker comes off the pole. We cruise along the shore, round the lighthouse at 1600, and drop the hook outside Matthew Town. Spicy dinner at Pride of Great Inagua and back to the boat at midnight.

Monday, August 10: I fill our water cans and check the weather while my crew plays on the beach. Willie and Richard drag aboard a bag of shells they collected, and we depart under sail at 1800. Cathy takes the first watch, spots six ships. We are crossing the New York-Colón lane.

Tuesday, August 11: Rain comes in hard with thunder and lightning during Gail's watch. It clears by dawn and starts heating up. No wind. I put up the awning and motor till 1800, when we get a light breeze. Kids are getting restless.

Wednesday, August 12: Thunderstorms all night, with wind on the nose. Favorable easterly comes in at 0700, but two hours later we're becalmed off the coast of Cuba. Gail makes biscuits in hot cabin. Kids are fighting and fussing. It's pretty cramped with this many on the boat. Tanned bodies are stretched out all over the place soaking up sun. There's nothing else for them to do. Breeze comes in at 1600, and back up goes the main and genny. We pick up Cape Verde light at 2000. Cathy takes the first watch and falls asleep in the cockpit.

Thursday, August 13: I set the spinnaker at 0800 and drop it at noon when our easterly dies. Sun line puts us 190 miles out of Miami. I'm anxious to get there in a hurry after hearing weather report on radio. A hurricane may be developing around 18° N, 62° W, near St. Thomas. Still a depression, it's not expected to turn into a storm overnight. Gail takes the first watch in a light squall.

Friday, August 14:

Early breakfast of eggs and bacon. I listen for the latest on the depression. It's coming up pretty rapidly, but I don't think we are in any trouble. A breeze in the afternoon gets us moving after our usual midday calm. At dark we see the loom of lights on the horizon. We're too far out for it to be Miami, but an RDF check says it is. I rework my noon sun line to see where I went wrong, discover I had plotted it as if we were in the Southern Hemisphere. That and the kick of the Gulf Stream puts us 30 miles closer than anticipated. Who's complaining?

Saturday, August 15:

It is 0400. My crew is asleep. *Molly Brown* is tied up in the same Miami marina she departed from a year ago. She has crossed her track. I pour myself a drink. Cheers.

EPILOGUE

Having circumnavigated the world, thereby fulfilling requirements for membership in the "After You, Magellan" society, I could have taken a bus to Annapolis, and my accomplishment would not have been diminished. Certainly everything had to be anticlimactic from here on in. Or so you would expect. But it didn't work out that way. On the very same day we arrived in Miami, I almost sank *Molly Brown* in the Intercoastal Waterway. It happened like this:

After an early breakfast, we refueled and headed up the waterway, stopping in Hollywood for lunch. I tied the boat to the bulkhead with a genoa sheet. We dawdled here a few hours, the kids taking a swim, Gail and I taking a nap under the awning. Perhaps I wasn't entirely awake when it came time to leave, for after untying the genoa line, I left it trailing in the water. Shortly after getting underway, the sheet fouled the propeller, killing the engine. Once I figured out what the trouble was, I put on the mask, grabbed another genoa sheet to hang onto in the fast current, and jumped into the water. I unwound the line from the propeller and flung it over the side. Then I climbed aboard, and we were off again. But I had forgotten something—the other sheet. It was now dragging.

I discovered the blunder in Fort Lauderdale at the 17th Street drawbridge. As we neared the span, I noticed a sign stating that it opened on the hour and half-hour. Since it was now a quarter-past five, I reversed the prop so we could back off and mark time. The dangling line immediately wrapped itself around the propeller, and again the engine stalled. Out of control, the boat swung sideways as the current swept it toward the bridge. I began blowing the horn, but it didn't do any good. The operator wasn't about to open the bridge, with bumper-to-bumper traffic on it. Just before we hit I thought, here's where I lose the mast. It smacked the bridge hard, snapping a shroud, but didn't break. Instead it bowed like a fishing rod, causing *Molly Brown*, straining against the current, to heel over so far that water spilled into the cockpit. Yelling for Gail to get the life jackets on the kids, I tossed the bow line to a powerboat that raced to our aid. The boat tugged on the line to no avail. The current was too strong. There was one consolation: If *Molly Brown* went down, there were plenty of people to fish us out. We had drawn quite a crowd. Happily, that wasn't necessary. The drawbridge finally opened, freeing the mast, and the yacht righted herself. A powerboat pulled us over to the Americana marina, where we sat for a couple of days while repairs were made.

Tuesday morning we headed out into the Gulf Stream. There, at least, we would have no drawbridges to contend with. We would also have no air, I soon discovered, which meant we had to motor. And we did until Thursday afternoon, when *Molly Brown* ran out of gas. I had forgotten to refuel in Fort Lauderdale. As we flopped around under a hot sun, I plotted our position— 150 miles out of Cape Fear, 240 out of Morehead City. All we needed was a breeze. We got one after dinner. It was still blowing nicely next morning, and I decided to try for Morehead. Flying the spinnaker and riding the Gulf Stream, *Molly Brown* was clipping along at a good ten knots. We stood watches that night, Willie taking over from me at 6 A.M. It was daylight then, and as long as we kept our easterly heading there was nothing to worry about. But, I cautioned Willie, if you have problems don't hesitate to wake me. Thirty minutes later he was yanking on my arm. *Molly Brown* was aground. It wasn't Willie's fault. I told him to steer east, and he did—right up onto the sand. We were closer to the inlet than I thought. A fishing boat pulled us off, and we worked into Morehead, getting there at nine o'clock. I called my sister to tell her we would be in Annapolis tomorrow. She promised a proper reception. We rounded Thomas Point at noon, sailing into a flotilla of 15 or 20 boats, all sounding their horns. It was deafening but beautiful. The moment I stepped off *Molly Brown* somebody stuck a cold beer in my hand, and for the next few hours I was not permitted to be empty-handed. Family, friends, strangers just happening by—all joined in to give us one hell of a homecoming. A newspaper reporter even showed up. But I was too overwhelmed to say much about the trip. When a yacht club acquaintance walked up and asked me what was new, all I could think of was, "Nothing much, really. What's new with you?" And he told me.

The Hartmans reclaimed their daughter and got Gail and me as a bonus. We would stay at their place on Spa Creek until I got squared away. I moved *Molly Brown* up that evening and tied her next to Ed Hartman's boat.

The following morning, while Gail and I were having coffee with Pat Hartman, I glanced out the kitchen window and saw a Coast Guard cutter coming up Spa Creek. How strange, I thought; I had never seen a Coast Guard cutter in Spa Creek before. She must be after something. Suddenly I knew exactly what she was after. I excused myself and walked out the back door and down the grassy slope to the bulkhead where *Molly Brown* lay. By the time I got there, Guardsmen were lashing her to the side of the cutter. A middle-aged man with closely trimmed hair and wearing civilian clothes was in charge. I asked him what was going on, although I felt reasonably certain I knew. He said he was agent Green from the Internal Revenue Service seizing my boat for nonpayment of $19,300 back taxes. I asked if he would grant me time to raise the money. He said he would give me an hour. I returned to the house and called Billy. Was it possible for me to raise $20,000 in an hour? The answer to that one didn't surprise me either. He doubted if I could raise $20 in an hour.

The agent wouldn't extend the time, but he allowed us to remove our personal belongings. Gail and Cathy came down and gathered up their clothes. I didn't have much—a pair of jeans, a T-shirt or two. I wrapped them in my old army blanket and looked around to see if there was anything else worth taking. My gaze fell on the log lying on my bunk. It was open to the last entry, a mere date— Sunday, August 23. I hadn't found the time to jot down the events of yesterday. Now it didn't matter. I flipped the log shut and tucked it under my arm. Then I walked up the hill and into the kitchen and finished my coffee.

Appendix

Recipe for fried tomatoes, southern Maryland style:
 Use green firm tomatoes, preferably home-grown. Supermarket tomatoes are good only for throwing at cats that howl in the night. Slice the tomatoes, dust them with flour, and salt and pepper them. Then fry them in hot bacon grease until they're crispy. You can serve them at any meal and not go wrong. I enjoy them particularly at breakfast with eggs, country ham, and grits. A friend of mine likes them with maple syrup. I think he's from Vermont.

Kyle

Dick

John

Connie

Maryrose